PROBLEM-POSING WITH MULTICULTURAL CHILDREN'S LITERATURE

Rethinking Childhood

Joe L. Kincheloe and Janice A. Jipson
General Editors

Vol. 31

PETER LANG
New York • Washington, D.C./Baltimore • Bern
Frankfurt am Main • Berlin • Brussels • Vienna • Oxford

ELIZABETH P. QUINTERO

PROBLEM-POSING WITH MULTICULTURAL CHILDREN'S LITERATURE

Developing Critical Early Childhood Curricula

PETER LANG
New York • Washington, D.C./Baltimore • Bern
Frankfurt am Main • Berlin • Brussels • Vienna • Oxford

Library of Congress Cataloging-in-Publication Data

Quintero, Elizabeth P.
Problem-posing with multicultural children's literature: developing
critical early childhood curricula / Elizabeth P. Quintero.
p. cm. — (Rethinking childhood; v. 31)
Includes bibliographical references and index.
1. Critical pedagogy. 2. Early childhood education—Curricula.
3. Multicultural education. 4. Children's literature—Study
and teaching (Early childhood). I. Title. II. Series.
LC196.Q87   370.11'5—dc22   2003019594
ISBN 0-8204-6738-3
ISSN 1086-7155

Bibliographic information published by **Die Deutsche Bibliothek**.
Die Deutsche Bibliothek lists this publication in the "Deutsche
Nationalbibliografie"; detailed bibliographic data is available
on the Internet at http://dnb.ddb.de/.

Cover design by Dutton & Sherman Design

The paper in this book meets the guidelines for permanence and durability
of the Committee on Production Guidelines for Book Longevity
of the Council of Library Resources.

Printed in the United States of America

This book is dedicated to the children and their families, the teacher education students and master teachers, and all my educator friends from whom I have learned so much over the years. Especially, I thank my most important teachers, my sons, Guillermo, Alejandro, and Rafael.

CONTENTS

ACKNOWLEDGMENTS

Several permission holders have generously given permission to use the following material: Roseann Lloyd, *Because of the Light*, Holy Cow! Press, 2003. Reprinted by permission of the author and publisher. All rights reserved; Francisco X. Alarcón, *Laughing Tomatoes and Other Summer Poems*. Text © 1997 by Francisco X. Alarcón. Reprinted with the permission of the publisher, Children's Book Press, San Francisco, California.

·1·

PERSPECTIVES OF POSSIBLITY

W e are living in a time of a consciousness of paradox. Many of the values of childrearing, education, and living are being called into question. Yet, of course, we have to keep on learning and keep on dreaming. At an event in New York City in early October 2001, White (2002) implored artists to "create as if your life depends on it; act as if the lives of others depend on it."

This seems to be good advice to us all, and as I reflect upon the many children I have known over the years as they interact with their friends, using their imagination and their stories, I realize that this is what they do; they create as if their lives depend on it; and they act as if the lives of others depend on it. We have a lot to learn from children while at the same time, as early childhood educators, we have a huge responsibility to provide reinterpreted, updated information for them as they grow and develop.

In Faith Ringold's *Tar Beach* and *Aunt Harriet's Railroad*, the character, Cassie, uses her imagination and her stories which nourish her to overcome oppression and limitations. In a *New York Times Book Review* (9/30/01) Margo Jefferson wrote,

> " . . . good fiction gives us the only real escape. It gives us pleasure—joy even— and it keeps us asking questions and disdaining pat answers. Real art matters now—the lyric, the epic, the satire, the memoir and the essay. In *The Nation*, Edward Said had written that intellectuals should work like artists, accepting "overlapping yet irreconcilable" realities. What is more difficult than to "truly grasp the difficulty of what cannot be grasped, and then go forth to try anyway"?

Children, through their play, especially when immersed in an environment of literature and art, can provide us with voices and perspectives of possibility.

Richard Rothstein (9/19/01) wrote in the *New York Times* shortly after the attack on the World Trade Center that while school reformers promote critical thinking, there is a question about what that means on a practical level. He said that teachers need to answer questions from students about personal safety, about what motivates others to attack us, about how we should relate to fellow citizens who are Muslim or Arab and about whether civil liberties should be curtailed in a time of crisis. He said that if unasked, these questions should be provoked. Few teachers are prepared to do this. Consequently, they will have to search for thought-provoking material, suitable (or convertible) for students in all grades.

The following week, Rothstein (9/26/01) wrote about examples of intolerance and told of teachers reminding students about the study they had done of many cultures that make up this nation. Literacy instruction in elementary school often uses readings from the works of authors from ethnic minorities to help pupils identify with characters and know about other perspectives. At a school in Providence, Rhode Island, one African-American girl at the high school urged military restraint. "In class," she argued, "they keep on saying that the bigger person is the one who walks away from a fight, the one who wants peace. How many people do we have to kill to make Americans feel better? Some of these politicians who want war are acting younger than we are."

Yes, we have much to learn from our students.

I believe that by using a problem-posing, critical literacy approach with children's literature, even the complex issues of a world in conflict and confusion can be addressed in an ongoing dialogue. Children's literature author, Lunge-Larsen (1999), reminds us of the importance of literature in children's lives in the introduction to one of her children's literature books,

> Over and over again, in wonderful, fanciful stories these themes (of being human) are repeated in a predictable formula that exactly mirrors the child's view of the world. Children, like the heroes and heroines in these stories (folk tales) perceive their lives to be constantly threatened. Will I lose a tooth? Will I be invited to play? Will I learn to read? By living a life immersed in great stories and themes, children will see that they have the resources needed to solve life's struggles. And, while listening to these stories, children can rest for a while in a world that mirrors their own, full of magic and the possibility of greatness that lies within the human heart. (p. 11)

Rosenblatt (1995) categorizes readers' involvement in text along a continuum. One end of this continuum is aesthetic reading, when a reader becomes involved in the story and identifies with the characters. At the other end of the continuum is reading to gain information. Of course, children operate all along the continuum and use books for enjoyment and learning.

Joseph Tobin (2000) documents that children are critical observers of media, of print, and of the world around them (including the adults they interact with). By weaving cutting-edge approaches such as poststructuralism, performance theory, and critical theory into his analysis, he demonstrates how the meanings children give to media messages depend on the local contexts in which they live. He shows the ways in which children can resist, parody, and appropriate the images and narratives of film, using local experiences to interpret global texts.

My own research (Quintero, 2001) documents children responding to literature in critical ways. Problem-posing teaching using children's literature nourishes an integrated curriculum which supports young children's meaningful learning. This method encourages integrated learning that is both developmentally and culturally meaningful through interacting with story, reading literature, and participating in related learning activities. The problem-posing method was developed by Paulo Freire (1973) and critical pedagogists going back to the Frankfurt School of Critical Theory in the 1920s, initially for use with adult literacy students. The method leads students of any age, experience or ability level to base new learning on personal experience in a way that encourages critical reflection. All activities focus on active participation.

This method has not been widely used with younger learners, but lends itself well to integrated early childhood learning. This book documents different groups of teacher education students as they experience the method in their classes and then as they use the method with young children. They practice combining theory with practice using this critical literacy framework for focusing on multicultural children's literature and creating contexts for integrated curriculum for early childhood. I use this method with the teacher education students I work with, and they use the problem-posing process with all ages of young children. Maxine Greene (1996) advises,

> As we devise curriculum and work on curriculum frameworks, it seems important to hold in mind the perspective, the possible. This means encouraging the kind of learning that has to do with becoming different, that reaches toward an open future—toward what might be or what ought to be. (p. 131)

What Is Curriculum?

The word "curriculum" comes from a Latin word that means to run a race. Now, in contemporary educational circles, people generally think of the curriculum as "the course to be run," which suggests that it is not the actual running, but the plan for the race. Others (Ely, 2003) argue that curriculum is not the plan or the recipe for the plan, but is, in fact, what transpires in the teaching and learning context for learners individually and as a part of the classroom community. Besides worrying about the definition, we educators struggle with how curriculum is developed. Especially in times of expensive, one-size-fits-all, prepackage curriculum kits, teachers who want to be the intellectuals (Giroux, 1988) they have studied for years to become, find that this task becomes crucial.

Teacher education programs are scampering to respond to the push by state boards of teaching and other credentialing bodies for "more content-area" knowledge in each of the teaching fields—including Early Childhood Education. However, those of us who have spent years in the early childhood classroom participating with toddlers, preschoolers, and first and second graders, and those of us who continue to review both the new research and the wisdom of our predecessors, worry. We worry that children's and families' cultures will be dismissed, we worry that play will not be valued, we worry that the policy-makers and curriculum developers who haven't "been there" will push inappropriate content on the young ones. At the same time, we want young children to have the benefits of exposure to people, places and ideas that enrich their worlds and stimulate their potential. And yet, most of all, we want to ensure that the children know that their family, their communities, and their schools support their learning.

Rationale

For decades early childhood educators have worked toward an understanding of supporting the development of what we call "the whole child." This term has come to mean a commitment to the recognition that cognitive development, social development, emotional development, and physical development are integrated in unique ways in each individual child influenced by both nature and nurture. We know the importance of viewing childhood as inquiry rather than a prescription in order to encourage a broader, less linear view of development and therefore, more inclusive strategies of care and education (Mallory & New, 1994). And, as global societies have become more and more interwoven, we strive for pluralistic programming. We also strive for a better understanding of how early childhood programs can support the sociocultural knowledge and experiences the children bring to our early childhood programs while we provide instructional experiences that prepare the children for success in school and life in the cultural context of the United States.

It is our responsibility as educators to challenge the sanctity of a single "early childhood western lens, the over reliance on child development paradigms, psychology, and the exclusive western ways of seeing the world" (Soto, 2000). For many years, early childhood educators looked to research to better understand patterns of development in order to improve teaching, teacher education and childhood. Currently, however, much research challenges the idea of child development through ideas that examine "development-in-context" (New, 1994) or the social, cultural, and economic factors that influence development (Lubeck, 1994).

Cannella (1997) gives a personal account of how she moved from a determinist Piagetian perspective to a postmodern philosophy regarding early childhood education. She, among others, believes that the construction of knowledge is rooted in power relations (Cannella, 1997). She traces the genealogy of childhood education and reminds us that childhood did not exist during the medieval period. She goes on to show the dramatic connection between historical and social context, including the power brokers of a given society at a given time, and the accepted notions about childhood.

In my work with immigrant and refugee families, I remember discussions with Hmong women describing their own "childhoods" in refugee camps in Thailand and Somali women describing family life in East Africa during the past decades. I would say that the "childhood" experience of these families is very different from many families in the United States and Western Europe and many other countries. Cannella (1997) believes that the knowledge base used to ground the field of early childhood education actually serves to support the status quo, reinforces prejudices and stereotypes, and ignores the real lives of children She says that "learning is only recognized and legitimized if it falls within what is conceptualized as developmentally appropriate. The pedagogical determinism is most certainly complete" (pp. 131–132). Cannella's (1997) work raises questions in terms of social justice and early education. Her questions include: How do we eliminate the two-tiered system? Does the curriculum respect the multiple knowledge and life experiences of younger human beings from diverse backgrounds? All discourses are dangerous (Foucault, 1983), especially without continued examination no one has focused on narratives that represent the voices of those who are younger, sights from which to view the impersonal forces that play roles in the construction of who we are and how our life alternatives are defined (Sawicki, 1991; Cannella, 1999, p. 37).

An early childhood teacher who puts these ideas into practice is Mary Tacheny, a first grade teacher in St. Paul, Minnesota. She works with Southeast Asian immigrant children and their families and shares the following thoughts.

> I think one area that has really helped strengthen me in taking risks in curriculum has been embracing an integrated approach, and interdisciplinary strategies. For example, . . . You don't have to be "married to a manual," you don't have to

take the curriculum and follow every scope and sequence activity. There are things that I can do to put together the objectives that are more appropriate to the needs of the students in my classroom and not let the manual dictate that. It's well worth the risk to go beyond that and to extend curriculum by embracing an integrated approach. My students write to state senators, they have written to a judge for example. It is overwhelming the responses they get. I have had a state senator come and meet my class based on their letters. We've been invited down to the Ramsey County Court House by a judge. Whether they are first graders or third graders they really respond when children write genuinely from their hearts.   (Tacheny, in Rummel & Quintero, 1997, pp. 156–15)

My Work, My Passions, My Biases

I am a qualitative researcher with a perspective about early learning and literacy which frames the ways I work and conduct research with all ages of learners from many different backgrounds. I research issues of early childhood education, families "at promise," language and critical literacy in the context of home culture and culture of learners' new learning environments in both schools and communities. I use a post-formal perspective which includes critical theory, feminist theory, and social, autobiographical narrative. This perspective (Kincheloe & Steinberg, 1997) demands that the politics of knowledge and the origins of sustained inequities of modern society be examined. Such a perspective grants us a new conception of what "being smart" means. "Postformalism is concerned with questions of justice, democracy, meaning, self-awareness, and the nature and function of social context" (Kincheloe, 2000, p. 83). I believe this must begin as we design and implement programs for the youngest of learners

I use problem-posing and critical literacy for literacy instruction for children, preservice teachers, and more advanced practicing teachers and graduate students. This problem-posing, often described as critical pedagogy, combines reflective thinking, information gathering, collaborative decision making, and personal learning choices. Teacher researchers and others who have designed self-reflexive research designs that attend to children's meanings of experiences (Davies, 1993; Dyson, 1997) have struggled with the issues of creating new contexts for learning and documenting the interactions in authentic ways. By using problem-posing, with its reflective and personal components, the learners are participating in a complex form of autobiographical narrative. I believe this combined approach allows students to move beyond a neutral conception of culture in discussions of their relationship between schools and families and toward a better-defined conception of culture in a pluralistic, multicultural society (Willis, 1995).

Problem-posing Critical Literacy

The problem-posing method, based on a critical literacy perspective, is powerful because it situates the participant as the activist in the dance between lived experience and new information. Problem-posing focuses on the process of question formulation, as opposed to Cartesian modernism/positivism's concern with question answering or problem solving (Kincheloe, 2001). Kincheloe (2001) reminds us that Einstein believed that question-formulation, or problem-posing, is more important than the answer to the question or the solution of a problem. The method encourages what I see as a natural movement from reflection toward action. Furthermore, the approach allows for multiple forms of authentic evaluation and assessment. I stress that I use this Listening, Dialogue, Action approach not as a prescriptive lesson planning format, but as a way to facilitate student choice and generative work which is related to students' lives whatever the age or context of the students.

I define critical literacy as a process of constructing and critically using language (oral and written) as a means of expression, interpretation and/or transformation of our lives and the lives of those around us.

Another related aspect of my rationale is feminist theory. Feminist theory has challenged many tenets of traditional knowledge as it is male-defined and practices in Western patriarchal cultures (Rogers, 1993). Through this feminist theory the learner seeks to include, rather than exclude, herself or himself in research and interpretation.

A teacher who combines both feminist theory and autobiographical narrative is Vicki Brathwaite, a teacher and reading specialist in the Brooklyn schools in New York. She constantly devises ways so that the cultural knowledge of her students and their families is included in her curriculum. She is always searching for books and children's literature that will help her students of diverse backgrounds feel pride in their own identity and heritage while they study the approved curriculum for their grade level. She says:

> My students like reading about people in other cultures, different countries and their populations and landmarks. A favorite book is *The Piñata Maker*. It is a Mexican nonfiction book it is a photo/essay of master piñata maker and it is in English and Spanish. The children love that book. They like books from their experiences. Children who are bilingual love books that are written in both languages

and speak of their experiences from their native country. Asian children love to identify with Omi Wong and other Asian books. Children love to identify with books and solve problems through characters in books. (Brathwaite in Rummel & Quintero, 1997, p. 127)

Through the Listening, Dialogue, Action process in the activities and readings, and reflection, the reader is participating in a complex form of autobiographical narrative. This combined use of literature and critical theory allows the readers to use autobiography as a way to move beyond a "neutral" conception of culture in discussions of the relationship between schools and families and move toward a more well defined conception of culture in a pluralistic, multicultural society (Willis, 1995). The students' participation in this method is autobiographical in the sense that the student is constantly encouraged to reflect on her/his own experience and autobiographical in the sense that the authors of the literature are giving us glimpses into their own autobiographies. Personal narrative lets us listen to the voices of the participants—students and authors, in their cultural contexts—as they tell about their experiences and explain ongoing efforts at agency and transformation. Bloch (1991) explains that this type of symbolic science ". . . focuses on intersubjectivities that are created through interactions between people, their discourse, and the interpretations of meaning within specific contexts" (Bloch, 1991, p. 97). This relational theory uses experience as central to theorizing and to understanding practice.

This participation is instructive for younger learners too. In cases with young children, a problem-posing approach can enrich and keep the student-centered integrity and provide the scaffolding needed for younger learners. This methodology, with its strong theoretical and philosophical underpinnings, encourages teachers not to limit their teaching to units and lesson plans. It encourages curriculum development to use a point of departure, the background funds of knowledge the children bring from their lived experience rather than from a written form of normalization. The method encourages integration of the community funds of knowledge, language and culture with the standard school curricula.

Problem-posing, Literature, and Early Childhood Integrated Learning

Early childhood programs based on culturally sensitive, child-centered, curriculum models and authentic and meaningful parent involvement are providing positive examples of programming for children and families across the nation. However, because of the changing needs of families and the persistence of western intellectual, psychological, and cultural perspectives, changes must continue to be made. Family childrearing practices must be supported and built upon to enhance social, emotional, cognitive, and physical development. Educators and parents must together determine appropriate early childhood programming that recognizes that the school's developmental milestones may be different from those of a cultural group with generations of different life experiences. Early childhood programs can build rapport through an informal, non-threatening environment, in which staff help parents to feel welcomed and comfortable so that they share the important sociocultural meaning in their lives. A problem-posing format using children's literature, especially multicultural children's literature, encourages collaboration and enhances multidirectional participatory learning. In other words, in this context, learning not only is transmitted from teacher to students, but teachers learn from students, and students from each other. We must ". . . search for intelligence where one has previously seen only deficiency" (Kincheloe, 2000, p. 81).

I believe that an integrated early childhood learning using a problem-posing format helps us find ways to look at alternative ways of knowing and people's real experiences and real achievements. Alternative ways of knowing that are represented by minority parents and children are not currently accepted in most school curricula. This is a loss to the children who bring this knowledge with them to schools and to the children brought up with traditional, mainstream cultural knowledge. This is a loss to parents who want to pass on cultural traditions and ways of knowing and who find themselves fighting not only the school information, but also the issue of their children believing that the forms of knowledge of the home are as important as mainstream cultural knowledge. Furthermore, this is a loss to teachers, who could be opening new worlds of exploration to children and providing a bridge between the culture of the school and the culture of the home.

In a previous study of teachers (Rummel & Quintero, 1997) it was found that, for example, the metaphors coming from literacy experiences provided a mechanism for "remything." Living in the current complicated times, we are surrounded by the ruins of myths and metaphors that have lost their power to shape and animate our lives. All around us, we hear the cracking of old certainties. And yet, in the midst of our confusion and grief, a new mythology is being born. In this study (1998), the authors discovered that all the teachers in the study were involved in midwifing emergent mythologies. They were transforming their school classrooms into mytho-genetic zones: places where new myths and metaphors are born. They are vessels through which new mythologies are slowly emerging. These teachers faced with the need to recreate common mythologies did so at a young age. This "re-creation" happened during a critical reading of what they were learning and out of school.

Historically, much of humankind's most profound reflections have emerged in the form of story. Story is the way people learn with all the complexities of related issues in teaching, as in life, intact. Therefore, the danger of stereotypical oversimplification of issues is minimalized. This problem-posing method encourages students to experience and make conscious the transformations that often occur through the reading of and reflection on literature. I believe there is a strong connection between critical pedagogy and using literature in teaching because I see a natural outcome of reading literature as transformative action. I believe this natural outcome is not causal, but that metaphors enriched by reading and other creative activities, structure our thinking, our understanding of events, and consequently our behavior (Lakoff & Johnson, 1980). Many experiences could give rise to metaphors. More surely than anything else, we are defined by our stories—the cultural myths we hear from our earliest days.

At the same time we are defined by the way we "rewrite" the myths we hear. These transformations can happen as a result of interacting with story and poetry—not often the format of psychological discussions in the media or the academic press. I maintain that with the help of the authors of literature, learners of all ages can reflect upon issues and concepts in a profound way. James, Jenks, & Prout (1998) challenge teachers and researchers to pay attention to children's experiences and to what situations might mean for children, not for the purposes of evaluating them in accordance with adult goals, but for the ways they inform us about how our practices contribute to children's unequal status. These authors also criticize the emphasis current models of education put on reading and interrogating childhood as a text rather than an embodied and material performance. They call for inquiries that combine a focus on critically examining childhood with attention to children's lived experiences. Again, I do not want to impose my interpretation of the individual stories for the students, but the listening, dialogue, and action considers the student as an individual who is part of family and community.

Considering the use of children's literature, with an emphasis on multicultural literature, some educators maintain that literature is art and therefore we do not need to be concerned too much about historical accuracy. Other educators who see children's interaction with literature as an important factor in the students' creation of a knowledge base about people and the world, are adamant that the books used be historically accurate. Thus, an ongoing disagreement ensues about how to determine which books to use in classrooms with young children. Of course, there are documented, unarguable facts in many stories, yet of course, history is told by humans with their own perspectives and philosophies. By using a critical literacy and problem-posing approach with multicultural children's literature, the stage is set for critical discussion of all topics, and questions such as "Whose story is this?" and "What is left out of this story?" and "What might be another side to this story?"

We teachers create the context for learners to pose questions and encourage the consideration of the strengths of students and their families and the consideration of the barriers they face daily. This process, combined with the mutual respect which becomes generative in this context, provides support for transformative action on the part of parents, children, teachers, and community members.

Qualitative Research with Preservice Students and Practicing Teachers in Early Childhood Classrooms

This ongoing qualitative research study is about using problem-posing, critical literacy with multicultural children's literature in early childhood classrooms. I have collaborated with teachers in a variety of contexts whose classrooms are active, vibrant sites for critical literacy development and learning. My philosophy about research is reflected in a comment by Zellermeyer (2003), "I learned that if you don't do research with people and for people, you shouldn't do research." In this book I focus on examples from both early childhood and elementary teacher education students and practicing teachers' journeys through their study of: 1) critical literacy, 2) multicultural children's literature, and 3) integrated early childhood curriculum.

Theoretical Framework

As previously stated, I define critical literacy as a process of constructing meaning and critically using language (oral and written) as a means of expression, interpretation and/or transformation through literacies of our lives and the lives of those around us. All scholars and teachers do not agree about what critical literacy is. The need for the plural form—'critical literacies'—suggests, rather, that a diversity of curriculum interventions are in theoretical, practical and political contest with one another (Luke & Freebody 1996). Comber (1998) believes it is possible to identify some shared assumptions about critical literacy:

- that literacy is a social and cultural construction,
- that its functions and uses are never neutral or innocent,
- that the meanings constructed in text are ideological and involved in producing, reproducing and maintaining arrangements of power which are unequal.

This study is based upon a post-formal perspective which includes critical theory, feminist theory, and social, autobiographical narrative. This perspective (Kincheloe & Steinberg, 1997) demands that the politics of knowledge and the origins of sustained inequities of modern society be examined. In this broader context, further direction comes from critical theory (Freire, 1973), feminist theory (Rogers, 1993), and relational, social theory (Rogers, 1993) and the larger perspective of post-formal theory.

Methods

Data Collection and Analysis

The methods involved are participant observation, interviews, and collection of students' work samples. The data is then analyzed by categories dictated by the theoretical perspectives of a post-formal theory, critical theory, feminist theory, autobiographical narrative, and by the target learning areas of critical literacy, multicultural children's literature and integrated early childhood curricula.

The participants are teacher education students in a large urban university's teacher education program, teacher education students in a small Midwestern university, and various groups of practicing teachers in professional development situations. Some of the courses involve the study of young children's language development and the acquisition of literacy. Other courses study curriculum theory and development in early childhood education. Students explored the nature of language, language development, language diversity, early reading and writing development, and the deep connection of language and literacy to all areas of learning. Students explored theories of learning, language acquisition, literacy development, and curriculum development. Students continually connected theoretical knowledge with practical applications. From the outset the students were informed by the course syllabus that the foci of the courses was either critical literacy with a post-formal perspective or curriculum study with a post-formal perspective.

Class periods or professional development sessions are divided into components for study of language and literacy or various aspects of curriculum theory and development. There are discussions of readings in small groups of class participants. The discussions are then related to critical questions in a problem-posing format. Students participate in three aspects of a problem-posing format (Listening, Dialogue, and Action) as a partial requirement for course completion. This format lends itself to our processing complex course content in a way that values students' prior knowledge and current professional responsibilities. The theoretical framework underlying the pedagogy also demands a critical treatment of new information and a responsibility for using this information in an action format.

Findings

Findings, from interviews and observations of teachers whose classrooms are active sites of critical literacy and their written responses about the children they work with using problem-posing activities with literature, have begun to provide dynamic information about literacy education and integrated curriculum for early childhood education. The data analysis has supported the belief that in order to support critical early childhood education, we must look at various fields of study and various forms of lived experience and local knowledge as recorded through the arts, media, and all aspects of children's work.

Possibilities for Use of Book

Because the book documents an ongoing qualitative study of teachers using this method with multicultural children's literature, the text will provide a model to be used in the classrooms of adult teacher educators as they study infant, toddler, preschool, kindergarten, and students in grades one and two. The structure of problem-posing allows for consideration of research in child development, cultural and linguistic contexts, learning theory, strategies for teaching young children, and all the related aspects of early childhood teacher education as the learners move through the activities. Along with the problem-posing structures for the teacher education students are examples of use of the method with each age group of children. In each chapter of the book, there are problem-posing lessons using multicultural children's literature for the teacher education students. There are also problem-posing lessons using multicultural children's literature for varying ages of young children that the students and I have developed together and explored with children. The model also includes opportunities for guided research into cutting edge investigations in the fields of child development, family advocacy, and public policy.

In a teacher education class, in the Listening part of the class we may have an introduction by the teacher which includes social and historical information related to the topic of study and the age group of children focused upon.

There will be suggestions for individual reflective journaling by students to reacquaint themselves with their own past experiences. This also includes pre-reading activities for focusing purposes. Then, the students may listen to the various children's literature authors by reading a literature selection.

In the Dialogue part, the students dialogue with peers through small and large group discussions and they dialogue with themselves as they write responses to the readings or discuss other tasks given by the instructor.

In the Action part, questioning is encouraged as well as suggestions of options for action. Student questions generate further questions which begin to confront the world outside the classroom. Students may generate suggestions for observation activities in schools and at community events, suggestions for interviewing topics, and suggestions for individual and collective community action. The action section is an ideal context for prospective teachers to learn action research techniques and practice this teacher research during their time in the field. In speaking about teachers as collaborative researchers, New (1994) encourages teachers to be classroom ethnographers, conducting formal and informal observations of children at work and play; she encourages teachers to be epistemologists to hypothesize about and experiment with diverse strategies, materials and activities; finally, she encourages the role of teacher as anthropologist as teachers consider the interface between children's cultural heritage and individual development.

The problem-posing activities are recursive activities, not a lesson plan in a preconceived, rigid sequence. Sometimes action is need first, for the concrete experience it provides. Then reflection follows, relating the action, the stories, to the student's life and the student's choices for more action.

When this method of problem-posing with children's literature is used with young children, the approach can enrich and keep the student-centered integrity and provide the scaffolding needed for younger learners and others for whom the standardized curriculum is not working. This methodology, with its strong theoretical and philosophical underpinnings, encourages teachers not to limit their teaching to units and lesson plans. It encourages curriculum development to use a point of departure, the background funds of knowledge the children bring from their lived experience

In Chapter 2 Critical Literacy is explained in more detail with examples from teacher education students, practicing teachers, and young children of varying ages. Chapter 3 discusses in detail the ways home and community contexts of children point out the necessity for our considering all early childhood education in a multicultural context. Chapter 4 discusses infancy and toddlerhood and ways early childhood professionals may use problem-posing critical literacy and multicultural children's literature. Chapter 5 addresses preschoolers and their potential and use of problem-posing critical literacy and multicultural children's literature. Chapter 6 is focused on kindergarten students and Chapter 7 on first graders. Chapter 8 is about the second grade learning context and the possibilities of using legend, myth, and real writing and reading opportunities in exciting learning contexts—in spite of standardized curricula and skill development pressures. Chapter 9 goes back full circle to reconsider issues of critical literacy and how that relates to multicultural children's literature and early childhood curriculum.

Examples of Use of Method with Young Children

The following are examples of how to use problem-posing as a frame for early childhood integrated curriculum. It is important to note that the key to problem-posing is choice and relevance to student lives and contexts. The teacher may offer choice in the selection of literature pieces and in activity selections. The students' critical participation comes not only in the ultimate action taken after the readings, but in the sometimes tiny steps of choice built into the whole activity process. I include here two examples of problem-posing. One is a first grade classroom, and one is a Head Start classroom of three- and four-year-olds. Both of the examples are based on use of the book *The Whispering Cloth: A Refugee's Story*, written by Pegi Dietz Shea, illustrated by Anita Riggio, stitched by Youa Yang. These two examples using the same children's story show how a work of literature can be used with activities developed for varying age levels.

Example from a First Grade Class

The following observational case documents a lesson in a first grade classroom in an urban school in a large Midwestern city. The teacher is a twenty-year veteran teacher with the district, a woman of Irish American descent. The student teacher with her is a Hmong male who is from the community where the school is situated. The students in the class consist of sixteen Hmong children, three African American children, and one child from South America. For this lesson, the teacher used the storybook *The Whispering Cloth*, by Pegi Deitz Shea, illustrated by Anita Riggio, and stitched by Youa Yang.

Listening:
- The teacher began by gathering the children around her in the classroom center area where she unfolded several quilts. She reminded them of previous discussions and stories they had shared about quilts. Then she showed a weaving from Ireland and explained that it was from the

country her family came from. Then, she held up a large, colorful "story-cloth" which had been made by one of the school staff's relatives who is Hmong.

Dialogue:
The teacher asked,
- "Do you think a quilt could tell a story? Do you think you can hear a story from a cloth?" The children discussed briefly what they thought about the question.

Action:
- Then the teacher passed the folded cloth around the circle, so that each student could "listen" to the cloth. Then, she showed the class the book and told them just a little about the book. "It is a story about a Hmong girl and her grandmother who live in a refugee camp in Thailand. Grandmother is teaching Mai how to make storycloths and Mai creates one that tells her story." Then the teacher showed the bilingual glossary in the book with Hmong words and English translations, and explained that she would read the story in English in a few minutes, but that first, the student teacher would read it in Hmong.

Listening:
- The story was read in Hmong. The students who did not understand Hmong appeared to be fascinated by the words in spite of not comprehending.

Dialogue:
The teacher then asked,
- Can you guess what the story was about based upon Mr. Z's intonations, the pictures, and so forth?

Action:
- Then the teacher read the story in English.
- The student teacher explained to the students that he had written a letter to their families explaining what they were learning about. The letter was written in English, Hmong, and Spanish. In the letter, the teachers ask the parents if their child could either share a storycloth, quilt, or other artifact that tells a family story. When the items were brought to school, extension activities were implemented.
- The class made a class storycloth with a contribution from each student's drawing and writing (native language or English or both) during the following days.

Example from a Head Start Class

In preparation for the lesson using the storybook *The Whispering Cloth*, by Pegi Deitz Shea, illustrated by Anita Riggio and stitched by Youa Yang, the staff collected important props for the "centers" in the classroom. In the dramatic play area, there was a collection of traditional Hmong clothing and empty boxes of rice and other staple foods from the Asian grocery store, cooking implements used in traditional Hmong cooking, and a poster of a Hmong family working in their garden. In the block center there were a few tiny road signs with Hmong writing, some airplanes and some plastic farm animals. In the book center there were several storybooks of Hmong folktales, and a couple of class-made books written in Hmong and English by the mothers in the family literacy class. In a manipulative toy area there was the "generic" toy farm with the addition of Hmong dolls in traditional dress. In the science/sand/water area, the teachers have provided paper cups and potting soil and various vegetable seeds for the children to plant vegetables. In the art area small squares of burlap, blunt darning needles and yarn (and a parent volunteer at the station) awaited the children so that they could stitch a small story cloth.

Listening:
In this particular Head Start class, there are five Hmong children and twelve children from other backgrounds. First, the teacher gathers the group in the corner where they always have story time.

- She asks, "Does anyone know the country that Nou, PaDer, Moua, and Xeng's grandparents came from?" The children look around at each other and someone says "California" and then one of the Hmong children says, "No, Laos." The teacher says, "Yes, and this story is about a little girl and her grandmother who had to leave Laos to go to Thailand to the refugee camps because of the war." She then holds up a large story cloth that one of the mothers had made which depicted people farming their crops, then running from soldiers, swimming across a river and then gathering in a fenced "city." She asks the children about the different stitched representations and they give their ideas about what they mean. "Okay, let's listen to the story about Mai and her grandmother."
- She reads the story.

Dialogue:
- The teacher asks the children: Where did Mai's story that was stitched come from? Where did she and Grandma want to go when they saved

enough money to leave the refugee camp? Why was Mai sad about her mother and father? Did you like Mai's bed in her new house?

Action:
- Now the teacher explained all the different activities available at the centers and the children dispersed to play and work alone and with peers and parent volunteers.
- The following day a Hmong elder came in with a few traditional Hmong musical instruments to play for the children.

Conclusion

In conclusion, I believe that by adapting this problem-posing method for integrated early childhood curriculum, children have more meaningful opportunities for learning. I believe also that by documenting the children's growth, their strengths, their needs, and the interactions and transactions that occur in a positive early childhood context surrounded by story and multicultural literature, new pathways for significant research will emerge.

References

Alarcón, Francisco X. (1999). *Angels ride bikes and other fall poems: Los ángeles andan en bicicleta y otros poemas de otoño*. San Francisco: Children's Book Press.

Bloch, M.N. (1991). Critical Science and the History of Child Development's Influence on Early Education Research, *Early Education and Development*, 2 (2): 95–108.

Brathwaite, V. (1997). In Rummel & Quintero, *Teachers' reading/Teachers' lives*. p. 166. New York: SUNY.

Cannella, G. S. (1997). *Deconstructing early childhood education: Social justice and revolution*. New York: Peter Lang.

Comber, B. (1998). *'Coming, ready or not: Changing what counts as early literacy.'* Keynote address to the Seventh Australia and New Zealand Conference on the First Years of School.

Davies, B. (1993). *Shards of glass: Children reading and writing beyond gendered identities*. Allen and Unwin.

Dyson, A. H. (1997). *Writing superheroes: Contemporary childhood, popular culture, and classroom literacy*. New York: Teachers College Press.

Ely, M. (2003). Personal communication. New York: New York University.

Foucault, M. (Spring, 1983). Structuralism and poststructuralism: An Interview with Gerard Raulet. *Telos* 55, 195–211.

Freire, P. (1973). *Education for critical consciousness*. New York: Seabury.

Giroux, H. (1988). *Teachers as intellectuals: Towards a critical pedagogy of learning.* MA: Bergin & Garvey Publishers, Inc.

Greene, M. (1996). *Releasing the imagination: Essays on education, the arts, and social change.* San Francisco, CA: Jossey-Bass.

Harste, J., Woodward, V., & Burke, C. (1984). *Language stories & literacy lessons.* Portsmouth, NH: Heinemann.

James, A., Jenks, C. & Prout, A. (1998). *Theorizing childhood.* New York: Teachers College Press.

Kincheloe, J.L. (2001). *Getting beyond the facts.* New York: Peter Lang.

Kincheloe, J.L. (2000). Certifying the damage: Mainstream educational psychology and the oppression of children. In Soto, Lourdes D. (Ed.) *The politics of early childhood education,* pp. 75–84. New York: Peter Lang.

Kincheloe, J.L. & Steinberg, S.R. (1997). *Changing multiculturalism.* Philadelphia: Open University Press.

Lakoff, G. and Johnson, M. (1980). *Metaphors we live by.* Chicago: University of Chicago.

Lubeck, S. (1994). The politics of developmentally appropriate practice: Exploring issues of culture, class, and curriculum. In Mallory, B. & New, R. *Diversity and developmentally appropriate practices,* pp. 17–43.

Luke, A. & Freebody, P. (1996). Critical literacy and the question of normativity: An introduction. In S. Muspratt, A. Luke, P. Freebody (1996) *Constructing critical literacies: Teaching and learning textual practice.* 1–13 Creskill, NJ: Hampton Press.

Lunge-Larsen, L. (1999). *The troll with no heart in his body and other tales of trolls from Norway.* Boston: Houghton Mifflin Company.

Mallory, B. & New, R. (1994). *Diversity and developmentally appropriate practices,* pp. 65–83. New York: Teachers College Press.

New, R. (1994). Culture, child development, and developmentally appropriate practices: Teachers as collaborative researchers. In Mallory, B. & New, R. *Diversity and developmentally appropriate practices,* pp. 65–83. New York: Teachers College Press.

Quintero, E. (2001). Problem-posing with children's literature. Unpublished manuscript.

Ringold, F. (1991). *Tar beach.* New York: Crown Publishers.

Ringold, F. (1992). *Aunt Harriet's railroad.* New York: Crown Publishers.

Rogers, Annie G. (1993). Voice, play, and the practice of ordinary courage in girls' and women's lives. *Harvard Educational Review, 63* (3), pp. 265–295.

Rosenblatt, Louise M. (1995). *Literature as exploration.* New York: Modern Language Association of America.

Rothstein, R. (September, 2001). *New York Times.* New York.

Rummel, M.K. & Quintero, E.P. (1997). *Teachers' Reading/Teachers' Lives.* New York: SUNY.

Shea, Peggy D. (1995). *Whispering cloth: A refugee's story.* Honesdale, PA: Boyds Mills Press.

Spodek, B. & Saracho, O. (1994). *Dealing with individual differences in the early childhood classroom.* New York: Longman Publishing Group.

Soto, Lourdes D. (2000). *The politics of early childhood education*. New York: Peter Lang.

Tacheny, M.(1997). Mary Tacheny. In Rummel & Quintero, *Teachers' reading/Teachers' lives*, pp. 233–234. New York: SUNY.

Tobin, J. (2000*). Good guys don't wear hats: Children's talk about the media*. New York: Teachers College Press.

White, D. R. (October, 2001). *New York Times*.

Willis, A. (1995). Reading the world of school literacy: Contextualizing the experience of a young African American male. *Harvard Educational Review (65)*, 1, 30–49.

Zellermeyer, M. (2003). Lecture at New York University. New York: Steinhardt School of Education.

CRITICAL LITERACY IN EARLY CHILDHOOD LEARNING

In Chapter 1, I define critical literacy as a process of constructing meaning and critically using language (oral and written) as a means of expression, interpretation and/or transformation through literacies of our lives and the lives of those around us. Is it possible to think in these terms when thinking about the learning of very young children? Absolutely.

This book is about research findings, pedagogical method, and intent. Our cultural, human roots that we pass on to children are no longer neatly contained within borders. According to Clandinin and Connelly (1996), stories are the nearest we can get to experience, as we tell of our experiences. They say that the act of our telling our stories seems "inextricably linked with the act of making meaning, an inevitable part of life in a . . . postmodern world" and only becomes problematic ". . . when its influence on thinking and perception goes unnoticed" or is ignored (Goldstein, 1997, p. 147). Brady (1995) points out that, in identifying a politics of difference and identity, literacy is a central mechanism for discussing power, subjectivity, history, and experience. It becomes a way to translate these issues of politics into pedagogy.

As previously explained in Chapter 1, this problem-posing method leads students of any age, experience or ability level to base new learning on personal experience in a way that encourages critical reflection. All activities focus on active participation. Sometimes students who are unfamiliar with Freire's work at first are confused by the term "problem-posing." They ask if the method requires that there be a "problem." I then spend some time discussing the difference between calling something a problem and problematizing a situation or a set of ideas. The problem-posing comes from Freire's (1985) ideas about conscientization, which he defines as "the process by which human beings participate in a transforming act" (p. 106). He goes on to say that "conscientization thus involves a constant clarification of that which remains hidden within us while we move about in the world, though we are not necessarily regarding the world as the object of our critical reflection" (Freire, 1985, p. 107). The method encourages students to choose and examine voices in literature through poetry, fiction, academic research reports, and memory, focusing on authenticity of multiple experiences in multiple contexts.

Drawing on the notion of moving from reading, to interpretation, to criticism, Appleman and Green (1993) show the value of teaching high school students theoretical perspectives: reader-response, structuralist, Marxist, and feminist critical approaches. When providing students with critical theory, Appleman found that, particularly with feminist and Marxists perspectives, student acquired a critical vocabulary that resulted in insightful interpretations of literature. She also found that, although the students' understanding these theoretical perspectives remained somewhat superficial, having a theoretical orientation enhanced their confidence in articulating and sharing their responses in the classroom. My students lead themselves and their peers a step farther than classroom response: criticism to action. I, student teachers, and the teachers I have worked with, have found this movement to action happens with younger learners also.

As I have observed children over many years, I have seen them engage in critical literacy in astounding ways. When I was observing bilingual four-year-olds and collecting data for my dissertation, I had lessons from Valencia (all names in this book have been changed) about ways to use critical literacy in advocating for herself and her mother in a difficult domestic situation. I also had lessons from Carla about ways she used critical literacy to negotiate roles for work and play within her family.

Problem-posing teaching using children's literature nourishes young children's meaningful learning. This method encourages integrated learning that is both developmentally and culturally meaningful through interacting with story, reading literature, and participating in related learning activities.

This problem-posing, often described as critical pedagogy, combines reflective thinking, information gathering, collaborative decision making, and personal learning choices. By using problem-posing, with its reflective and personal components, the learners are participating in a complex form of autobiographical narrative. I repeat that this is important because the approach allows students to move beyond a neutral conception of culture in discussions of their relationship between schools and families and toward a better-defined conception of culture in a pluralistic, multicultural society (Willis, 1995). A problem-posing format using children's literature, especially multicultural children's literature, encourages collaboration and enhances multidirectional participatory learning. In other words, in this context, learning not only is transmitted from teacher to students, but teachers learn from students, and students learn from each other. Problem-posing helps us find ways to look at alternative ways of knowing and people's real experiences and real achievements.

When I begin working with a group of teacher education students, adults, about issues of critical literacy, I begin with a short history of Freire's work in literacy around the world. They find it easy to understand the use of the method and its theoretical underpinnings with adults. They find it harder, in some cases, to understand how the method may be used with young children and how the concept even relates to young children's learning. Here, Grace enters to help me.

As a way to present examples of children using critical literacy, I use the storybook, *Amazing Grace* by Mary Hoffman in a problem-posing format. This helps adult students begin thinking and working with critical literacy for young learners.

Listening:
- Close your eyes and imagine yourself as a character in one of your favorite stories or as a painting or other work of art. What do you look like visually? Where are you? What are you doing? What is going on around you? Are you saying anything? Draw a sketch or write a self-portrait beginning with "I am . . ." and include as much detail as you can about what you imagined.
- Now, write about a situation in which some said you couldn't do something you really wanted to do. Did you do it anyway and prove that person wrong? How did you do it? Or did you take the advice? Why?
- Listen to the story *Amazing Grace*, by Mary Hoffman.

Dialogue:
- Discuss what happened in the story. Discuss how the story of Grace relates to what you wrote previously about your own story.

Action:
- Choose one of the possible actions to complete and report about next class meeting.
  1. Observe a child or group of children in your field site classroom and document an example of them using critical literacy. What happened? What did they do? What did they say? What was the transformative action?

2. Document an adult demonstrating or supporting a child using critical literacy in a community or home context.
3. Reflect and write about an example of your own use of critical literacy in your own life. What happened? What did they do? What did they say? What was the transformative action?

Concurrently with the discussion about critical literacy with young children, I often present the urgently important and related information about language acquisition and multilingual learners. This is because culture, family and language are inextricably tied to critical literacy by their very nature.

Culture, Family, and Language and Critical Literacy

Issues of language and literacy in all classrooms have the potential to enlighten all students about meaning from a variety of perspectives. By the year 2030 over half of students in schools in the United States will be students of multicultural and multilingual backgrounds. For English Language Learners the context of home culture and culture of their new learning environments in both schools and communities are important for all teachers to consider. The use of native languages while learning English and a variety of other topics helps students express their voice in oral and written ways (Torres-Guzmán, 1993).

Acculturation and language acquisition are impacted by the process of aligning new societal expectations and requirements with previous cultural norms, individual perceptions, and experiences preeminent in immigrants' lives. Yet, these urgent issues are often ignored (Ullman, 1997; Zou, 1998). Franken (2002) reports research documenting that when students are faced with a topic on which they have little content and domain-specific knowledge, interaction is significantly helpful for understanding text. By virtue of the fact that many immigrant students come from such a variety of backgrounds with such different "funds of knowledge" as Moll (1987) reports, it is almost inevitable that many occasions will arise in the literacy classroom when one or more students have a lack of background knowledge on a topic.

All over the world critical literacy is being studied in terms of theory, practice, policy and research (Comber & Kamler 1997; Muspratt, Luke, & Freebody, 1997; Freire & Macedo, 1987). The widespread attention does not mean scholars agree upon the definition or the extent to which the theory and the practice can or should be separated. The issues of power, what students learn to read and write, and their access to transformative use of their literacy skills are exaggerated in the classroom contexts of multilingual learners.

Teacher Education Students Learning to See and Document Critical Literacy

As classes address literacy and curriculum issues through problem-posing and the use of multicultural literature, student responses reveal their understandings of the theoretical perspectives and practice of critical literacy. Initially, teacher education students rely upon the example of *Amazing Grace* to make their identifications of critical literacy being exhibited by young children.

One student wrote in her response journal about her experience observing a child using critical literacy:

> I am currently doing my first student teaching in a second grade class. L., who is one of the most hyperactive and talkative students, reminded me of Grace last week during our regular group meetings at the rug. We had a guest named Jane who was having a discussion with us about the Brooklyn Bridge. During the discussion, Jane asked the children if they had ever built something. L. raised her hand and told us that once she built a toy car for her little cousin. Brandon one of her classmates quickly said "Girls don't know that much about cars," but she told him that she knew many things about cars. L.'s attitude and the way she expressed herself at that moment reminded me of Grace's courage and personality.

Another student wrote:

> A few students in the classroom, where I student teach, are involved in an after school program where they will be performing a play adopted from Cinderelli, a favorite rhyme book of theirs. As seen in the story of *Amazing Grace*, interpretation of literature, use of imagination and role-playing are some fundamental elements students will have to understand and make use of during the preparation for their play.
>
> When the children make mention of their upcoming performance, their eyes light up and I can feel the excitement radiating from them. The passion these children have relates to the passion for books the author of *Amazing Grace* was trying to get across. It is the same passion for reading I have when I come across a book, so brilliant and extraordinary, that I cannot bear to put it down.

Another student wrote:

> I was sitting on the hard floor of the music room in my field placement school. Doe, Ray, Mes were filling the air, when suddenly the teacher introduced a new topic. She wanted one student to come up to the board and draw a small vertical line to denote the syllables of the words in each line of a very short song. No one raised their hand, except one small boy. He was not supported by his classmates, they believed that he could not do it, because they had been unwilling to try themselves. He walked up to the board filled with confidence and although he

made a few mistakes the music teacher praised him for trying. As I took notice of this scene I remember "Amazing Grace" and I thought that the premise was the same, that no one should keep you from trying.

Yet another teacher education student said:

> It was great to see and hear the story of *Amazing Grace* in class yesterday. In college we rarely have such opportunities. It was also interesting to see how one story was linked to the assignment we completed in class.
>
> In my field placement there is a student in my first grade class that I could also relate back to *Amazing Grace*. On my first day on site, my teacher informed me that there was a new student in the class. He has been admitted to the class just the previous week. When I asked her why he had come to school in the middle of the school year, I was in for a surprise. My cooperating teacher informed me that he was a case of child abuse, who was also being neglected, and therefore had late admission into school. This unfortunate incident relates to *Amazing Grace* because the student is not up to par for the first grade reading level, yet he is determined to catch up to the rest of the students. The teacher advised me to work with him the first two days of my student teaching experience. As I was working with him, I realized that he wouldn't keep down the book until he read and understood all the words in it; the teacher asked all the students to keep their books and meet on the rug. However, this boy insisted on keeping on reading and stretching out the words. Even though I have known him for two days, I could see the determination in him to strive to do his best and fulfill his goals, as Grace did. I look forward to working with this student for the rest of this semester and observing his progress and determination to be a successful reader.

And finally, another student who was working in a different school wrote:

> I am in a Kindergarten and the school is great. I really enjoy being there. The little girl in *Amazing Grace* reminds me of several of the children that I work with in my field experience. They are determined to spell and write, follow the rules, be good students, and accomplish as much as they can in a days time. I have helped several of them with their writing, reading, and spelling, and I am still amazed that they are able to do so much at such a young age.
>
> Currently, this Kindergarten class is working on "How To . . ." books. They choose something that they think they are good at, and then they write some steps out to tell someone else how to . . . do what they think they are good at. I think the "How To . . ." books are wonderful because it helps the children analyze themselves and look for things that they really like about themselves. Just like the little girl in *Amazing Grace*, there is an innocent kind of self-examination which encourages the students that they can accomplish real things. So far, I have seen, of the many books in progress, "How to . . ." books on ice skating, watching TV, reading, writing, helping out Mom, riding a bike, and so much

more. I think they are great. I really enjoy helping them spell out their words and organizing the pages of their books.

As can be seen in the students' responses to the assignment and their new ability to tune in to critical literacy in young children, many issues and important questions began to arise about home language, bilingualism, learning academic English and related issues.

Last week I was walking around the classroom during independent writing time, when F.'s piece caught my eye. The title, "M E X I C O" was in bold letters that colorfully stretched across the top of the page. I stopped and I asked her if I could read it. She happily agreed. I noticed that Spanish and English intermingled throughout the whole piece, quite an accomplishment for a second grader. Some of the words were written in Spanish, with the English words in parenthesis: "My tio Jose (Uncle Jose) pick us up at the aeropuerto Mexican (Mexican Airport). I was very impressed by her usage of Spanish words within an English sentence. She had the great insight to put the English words in parenthesis. It was obvious that she wanted to share her knowledge of Spanish words, while not alienating non-Spanish speakers.

Another student commented on the relationship between some of the background knowledge reading information about language acquisition.

This article (Fostering Second language Development in Young Children, ERIC Digest) reminded me of my best friend's nephew Julian. Her parents are originally from Costa Rica. My friend and her older sisters all grew up speaking Spanish and English. Her sister married a man who also spoke both Spanish and English. When J. was born, different family members spoke to him in different languages. Now when I baby-sit him I noticed that he combines or mixes both languages when he speaks. The other day he was showing me one of his toys and he said, "This es mio." I knew he was trying to say "this is mine" or "Este es mio." I understand basic Spanish and therefore I don't find it difficult to understand J. when he switches from one language to another. At times it seems to me that he is confusing the two languages. However, some days J. seems to speak only Spanish and other days only English. The part of the article that I felt related to J. was the part about code-switching. J. was code-switching and using appropriate "critical literacies" in his world.

Another student talked about an example of critical literacy on her part.

Whenever my grandmother gets any mail that is in English, I read it for her and explain what it means. It makes no sense to me that some agencies or companies send their clients materials in a language that they cannot understand.

Whenever she is sent something that is either in Spanish or bilingual she is completely empowered. She knows how to read! Just not so well in English. I guess this would be an example of critical literacy.

Another student saw the relationship between language, literacy, and the transformative action of advocating for a student:

Last year, I was a voluntary teacher at my church. I taught a first year communion class every Saturday. It was the first time I was teaching but for some reason it felt like I had been there for years. Among my students, I had an eight year old named J. who most of the time never brought his homework. I was really concerned about him. I tried calling home a few times but nobody answered. I finally decided to write a letter to his mother. It was a tough situation because his parents were divorced and his father had him over the weekend. When I saw his father on Saturday after class and told him about my concerns and he always used to blame J.'s mother.

So I figured that maybe if I wrote a letter to his mom and explained what was going on things could change. I knew his mother spoke Spanish more than English so I wrote the letter in Spanish. In the letter I introduced myself and told her how happy I felt having her son as my student. I told her that I wanted to meet her and that I was really concern about J. I also told her my schedule and even wrote down my phone number so she could contact me. After sending the letter, one Saturday morning she came to visit me.

A student teacher talked about learning from and with an English Language Learner:

One ESL student is in my class. The first few times when I sat next to him during independent reading, he declined to read to me. At first I thought it might be a competence issue, that he didn't feel like his English was good enough. However, in viewing his writing and in catching little bits of his reading, he sounded fairly fluent.

So one day I decided to be persistent and just sat next to him while he was choosing books. He was going through one about energy and oil. I asked, as usual, if I could listen to him read. He said no, as usual, but this time I just didn't leave. I sat there and began probing why he didn't want to read. "Is it because you don't know the words? Do you need to make a better book selection? " He said, "No" to my questions, so I decided to take a different approach. I figured if he didn't want to read to me, at least if I got him to talk about the book, we'd still be doing some literacy work.

I asked him why he chose the book, what interested him about it. Eventually I discovered that he was looking for his home country of Czechoslovakia in the book. I attempted point #1 in the article of "encouraging bilingualism" by asking about his home country, what it was like there. Actually, he hadn't even lived there very long before his family moved to Canada and then to the US. I found out his parents were doctors or scientists and were eventually planning to move back to the Czech Republic. I asked what were some of the similarities and differences between the two countries and if he knew how to say different words in Czech.

Afterwards, I felt good about having gotten that far with J. I was glad that he even opened up to me.

Autobiographical Narrative Illuminating Importance of Critical Literacy

The autobiographical opportunities inherent in problem-posing critical literacy methodology encouraged another student to tie her personal family story to the learning situation of students learning English for the first time when they come to school.

Being an ESL kid myself, I saw the difference between my siblings learning English. Being the oldest, I never got much exposure to English before I started school and the only exposure I got was in school and I struggled. My brother who is only a year younger, didn't have as much of a struggle but also is better at acquiring new languages, so it was easier for him. I am sure some of my confident students have that gift as well. My sister who is four years younger than I am, had lots of exposure before she started school because she had me and my brother at home. She was frustrated that she couldn't speak English, so she picked up quickly and had no problems with speaking two languages when she entered school. In speaking to my mother, I was the only one who had to take ESL classes at school. So I believe environment beyond the classroom makes a huge difference.

Other students showed regret at the loss of home language and the implications of that loss including being unable to talk with treasured elders.

As a child I was not encouraged to cultivate my home languages of Spanish and Italian in school. So, at home I would refuse to speak anything other than English because I felt that was the "right way" because that is what everyone else in school spoke. As a result, similar to what the article (see Fillmore, 1991, "When learning a second language means losing the first") stated, I lost the ability to communicate well with my extended family. Sadly, I am unable to converse with my grandmother who speaks only Italian.

This also relates to the classroom I am currently student teaching in. There are a few students from different nations and the teacher is well aware of this. Every morning during "meeting time" the children read what is written on the board. In both in English and in another language (usually Spanish) the words "good morning" are written and read out loud by all. This is an example of one way teachers could cultivate and help students appreciate multilingualism. It shows acknowledgment and respect for other languages and cultures, but more importantly communicates that to the children.

Critical Literacy with English Language Learners

Another example of critical literacy and critical literacies was compiled with the help of a class of English Language Learners and their teacher. The school is in a large Midwestern city and in a neighborhood that is home to many recent immigrants. In this particular class, the majority of students were native speakers of Spanish, a few from the United States, and more from Mexico and Central America. There were a few Hmong speakers, one speaker of Burmese, and one speaker of Somali in the class. The class was a sixth grade class with students between ages of eleven and thirteen, but due to the fact that many of them were very recent immigrants and some had had as few as three years of formal schooling in their past situations, she had to be creative. The variety of ages, variety in proficiency of English language use, and variety of formal schooling experiences demanded that the teacher plan learning activities that were supportive of the students' level of background knowledge (of course, including their home languages) as well as current learning needs. Her experience with this group of learners, her risk-taking ability to use critical literacy with such a varied group, and the students' proficient participation in the lesson show the potential of the method in even the most difficult of teaching situations. Here she used problem-posing with personal oral storytelling, native language writing and English writing.

Listening:
- The teacher showed the class a photo of herself when she was seven years old and then pulled out a map of Minnesota. She showed them the small Northern Minnesota town where her own immigrant family (from the former Yugoslavia) lived when she was a child. Then she told a story of how when she was seven, her father lost his job on the railroad and there was no other work in their town. So the family decided to move to California. Her dad went first and saved money, and then sent for the family some months later. Her mother, with her four young children, flew on an economy flight leaving at midnight and arriving in California at dawn. "I still remember how impressed I was by the sight of the toy city below . . . and how happy my dad was to see us," the teacher explained.

- The teacher then showed the drawing she had made in four parts that visually told her story which was drawn on one large sheet of butcher paper.

Dialogue:
- Then, the teacher asked the students,
  "What are sentences to explain each of the pictures?" As the students responded, she wrote their responses on the paper under the pictures (They worked on keeping the story in past tense and had to learn a couple of new words like airport and toy).

Action:
- Teacher then gave students a lesson guide that included the following instructions:

Your Story Assignment

1. Draw 4 pictures that show the 4 parts of your story.
2. Write a story about your childhood in your 1st language. Write the story in the past tense.
3. Write the same story in English. Divide it into 4 parts to go with the 4 drawings.
4. Tell your story in English to 3 other students and 1 teacher.
5. Rewrite your story in the present tense.
6. Hand everything in to your teacher to get a grade.

This guide, along with the task required of reading their stories to others, satisfies an important component of providing opportunities for the development of academic English. Cummins (1994) outlines a framework for English Language Learners that highlights distinction between conversational and academic communication. He notes that persuading another person of one's point of view and writing an essay demands cognitively demanding skills necessary for academic language use.

What Happened?

In terms of expression, by using a theme of personal history narrative, the teacher gave all students an opportunity to be experts in the telling of their story. By encouraging a three-tiered approach of drawing, native language writing, and English writing, the activity gave opportunity for all students, regardless of literacy proficiency, to tell their stories. In most cases in each of the classes the students were more expressive in terms of the content and details of their stories when writing in their native languages or drawing.

In terms of interpretation, this use of native language in the learning process gives ample opportunity for the students to reflect upon and discuss with others their interpretations of events of their immigration. In addition, in the third stage of the activity, when they were using English and telling what they had written to a classmate, interpretation of the story based upon the language choices made became a very dynamic academic process.

Finally, in terms of transformation, in this type of activity the opportunities are great. Every immigrant and refugee has experienced a transformation by moving from one country and culture to another. Learning to negotiate the new culture and new language provides for daily transformations. And very specifically, by attending to their own development of English literacy and academic English the students are generating more opportunities for further transformation. In activities in which culture, power, language, prior knowledge and current dilemmas are addressed are the opportunities for transformation the greatest.

For example, in this class all students expressed their stories, interpreted them, and documented transformation in terms of their families' immigration experiences. In terms of their literacy skills, the teacher documented through field notes that there was a variety of evidence of growth, and the teacher being grateful that the activity pushed them "to think and write in more complex and meaningful sentences" than they had previously done. She commented that, "It was lots of fun, very interactive, and encouraged the students to think and speak in meaningful complex sentences. I'll definitely do something like this again!"

Another teacher who embodies critical literacy in her work with her first grade students is a teacher in St. Paul, Minnesota. Her critical literacy has become activism in the truest sense. She gives children experiences of leadership and opportunities for real participation such as writing to state senators. She works on a classroom climate that offers children the opportunity to question, where it is okay to make mistakes. She uses critical literacy and provides the opportunity for learning as Carol Edelsky (1990) promotes, "Learning is best achieved through direct engagement and experience . . . learners' purposes and intentions are what drives learning" (pp. 24–25).

Mary Tacheny (1997) says:

> One thing I have noticed about children with different backgrounds and diversity is that there isn't a lot of judging. I have seen a lot of empathy grow in children. The rally around each other when someone is low or has had a bad day, and the kids are kind of like, convey the message "Don't mess with my people, we're all in this together." They are good buddies.

I had one boy talk about his story from Cambodia. He was talking about how his mother saw one of her children killed and there was nothing she could do and she had to keep running with the baby or she might die too.

These divergent life experiences aren't something the kids would have seen even on TV. . . . If you happen to be reading a book with a cultural background and a child has connections, they show a lot of ethnic pride. . . . we should all realize that we have a lot of things in common and that we all have past histories. What we bring to the present and where we want to be in the future are parts of we are, but I think we are parts of each other's stories too. (p. 154)

In terms of critical literacy and her curriculum activities, she feels it is well worth the risk to go beyond and to extend curriculum by embracing an integrated approach. She feels strongly about taking risks in the area of assessment because of the benefit to her students. She says:

I could go home to my nice little quiet neighborhood and just tuck myself in, but I can't now because of what I know about my children's lives and different things about school. [I have] . . . to fight, fight not only for the rights of particular program but for equal rights for all children. Like right now with the governor and budget cutting in education. . . . If all anyone ever did was think about what was happening to themselves, collectively nothing would happen. I think we have to have these global eyes, these eyes that the children have, so that we can make a difference. As one person we are not going to, but if these little packs of kids can stand up for each other, we can. I mean, they are going to make the difference, and they are going to be the voice of the future. So, why would we want to squelch their voice now? They've got ideas! (p. 218)

So, is critical literacy just another teaching method to come and go? I maintain that it is not. In simple terms, the fact the underlying bases for critical literacy are participant respect, choice, ownership in learning, and transformation will make critical literacy relevant always. And children are wise. Listen to a report of how wise. A student wrote in her journal:

I enjoy listening to the students talk. I especially enjoy listening to them when they think I am not listening. That's when they speak from the heart. Last semester I had observed a 2nd grade class. This particular conversation took place in the classroom during the teachers prep time. The health teacher was conducting a lesson. I was seated a few feet away from the rug where the lesson was taking place and over heard a few students talking. It was two boys and a girl.

Boy 1: She don't even know my name. I am not doing this
Boy 2: I don't think she knows what she's doing. She didn't even bring her own stuff.
Girl: You better do it or she's going to write about you.
Boy 1: I don't like her
Boy 2: She don't want to be here anyways. [*sic*]
Girl: You better do it.

What I learned from this conversation is that children respect you when you show them some respect. Apparently this teacher had been working with them since September. It is now November and she hasn't taken the time to get to know their names. I must agree with the students. I didn't understand the lesson either. She didn't come to the class prepared and she was utilizing the class teacher's materials.

Educational Implications

Critical literacy through problem-posing helps us find ways to look at alternative ways of knowing and people's real experiences and real achievements. Alternative ways of knowing that are represented by parents and children are not currently accepted in most school curricula. This is a loss to the children who bring this knowledge with them to schools and to the children brought up with more traditional, mainstream cultural knowledge. This is a loss to parents who want to pass on cultural traditions and ways of knowing and find themselves fighting not only the school information, but also the issue of their children believing that the forms of knowledge of the home are as important as mainstream cultural knowledge. Furthermore, this is a loss to teachers, who could be opening new worlds of exploration to children and providing a "bridge" between the culture of the school and the culture of the home. I maintain that with the help of the authors of literature, learners of all ages can reflect upon issues and concepts in a profound way. James, Jenks, & Prout (1998) challenge teachers and researchers to pay attention to children's experiences. They call for inquiries that combine a focus on critically examining childhood with attention to children's lived experiences. The listening, dialogue, and action structure for literacy education considers the student as an individual who is part of family and community. We teachers create the context for learners to pose questions and encourage the consideration of the strengths of students and their families and the consideration of the barriers they face daily.

It is important to embrace critical literacy because then we as teachers can ask questions such as: What kinds of voices are heard in early childhood activities?

From what kinds of classrooms are those voices derived? Who has the right to speak and be heard? What are the political, social, and cultural forces that are affecting the students? Whom shall schools serve? What is legitimate knowledge? What is the teacher's right to intervene and to try to change a student's agenda? What are the tensions between form and freedom in teaching? How do students see what is happening? How do teachers see it? What is the difference?

References

Alarcón, F. X. (1997). *Laughing tomatoes and other spring poems: Jitomates risueños y otras poems de primavera*. San Francisco, CA: Children's Book Press.

Comber, B. & Kamler, B. (1997). Critical literacies: Politicising the language classroom. *Interpretations*, 30, pp. 30–53, English Teachers' Association of Western Australia, Western Australia.

Cummins, J. (1994). Lies we live by: National identity and social justice. *International Journal of the Sociology of Language*, 110, 145–155.

Franken, M. (2002) When and why speaking can make writing harder. In Ransdell, S. & Barbier, M. (Eds.) *New Directions for Research in L2 Writing*, The Netherlands: Kluwer Academic Publishers.

Freire, P. & Macedo, D. (1987). *Literacy: Reading the word and the world*. Granby, MA: Bergin & Garvey.

Hoffman, M. (1991). *Amazing Grace*. New York: Dial Books for Young Readers.

Moll, L. (1987). Change as the goal of education research. *Anthropology and Education Quarterly*, *18*(4), 300–11.

Muspratt, S., Luke, A., Freebody, P. (1997). *Constructing critical literacies: Teaching and learning textual practice*. Creskill, NJ: Hampton Press.

Torres-Guzmán, M.E. (1993). Critical pedagogy and Bilingual/Bicultural Education Special Interest Group update. *NABE News*, 17(3), 14–15, 36.

Ullman, C. (1997). Social identity and the adult ESL classroom. *Eric Digest*. National Clearinghouse on Literacy Education. October 1997, EDO-LE-98–01.

Willis, A. (1995). Reading the world of school literacy: Contextualizing the experience of a young African American male. *Harvard Educational Review (65)*, 1, 30–49.

Zou, Y. (1998). Rethinking empowerment: The acquisition of cultural, linguistic and academic knowledge. *The Teachers of English to Speakers of the Other Languages Journal*. Vol. 7:4. Summer.

·3·

LANGUAGE, LITERACY, AND CHILD-REARING IN A MULTICULTURAL WORLD

In 1963, Sylvia Ashton Warner wrote in *Teacher*,

First words are different from drawings only in medium, and first drawings vary from country to country. In New Zealand a boy's first drawing is anything that is mobile; trucks, trains and planes, if he lives in a populated area, and if he doesn't, it's horses. New Zealand girls, however, draw houses first wherever they live. (p. 28)

She then explained that based on that knowledge, she made a first reader for the children in her class. But, she found that ". . .Tongan children's first drawings are of trees, Samoan five-year-olds draw churches and Chinese draw flowers." She goes on to advise, "How good is any child's book, anyway, compared with the ones they write themselves?. . . It's the bridge from the known to the unknown; from a native culture to a new; and, universally speaking, from the inner man out" (Ashton-Warner, 1963, p. 28).

Of course, children are different and come to us with many differing experiences. In 2003, a teacher education student in a graduate program in New York City wrote:

I came from India when I was four and started kindergarten when I was five.

Neither one of my parents spoke English, so when I started school it was a difficult experience for me. I felt so different from the other children and wanted to quickly learn English so that I can be a part of their world. I would run home after school so that I could finally be in a world that was familiar to me, with language and customs I was an expert of. However, at the same time I was angry with my parents for not knowing and therefore not being able to teach me English. I felt very alone in my experience. When my mother would pick me up after school I would beg her to not speak to me in Hindi. I was embarrassed about who I was.

What a shame for a child to be embarrassed about who they are because of the fear of rejection and because of the pressure to assimilate and build a new, acceptable identity for the new world they are a part of.

I am glad that I quickly realized the gifts of being different. And it is sad to say that it wasn't the teachers that helped me, nor my parents. It was the other kids at school. You will meet kids who will reject you right away because you're different and then there are those kids who are intrigued and want to learn from you and about you. That makes you feel special.

We Are Families

In a research study of literacy teachers (Rummel & Quintero, 1997) we learned about these teachers' family histories and saw glimpses of what sociologists and anthropologists call "positive social context." In other words, the magic of what families across cultures do best—care for, attend to, and love each other, regardless of conditions—has a lifelong effect. The teachers in our study brought the effects of their own families to their relationships with their students and to their teaching. They showed us how positive it is when educators are informed by families' knowledge. Family knowledge and literacy are interwoven fabric of cultural practices. The art of this family knowledge and related literacy practice promotes strength, encourages nurturance, and supports risk-taking.

Many teachers, like many well-known writers and visionaries (Allen, 1992; Walker, 1990) talk about the importance of passing on stories by parents and grandparents. In our study (Rummel & Quintero, 1997) one teacher smiled as she reported that her West Indian grandmother passed on teaching through folk tales. She also spoke at length about her mother's influence on her reading, in terms of modeling, interest, and actually providing trips to bookstores and libraries. Another teacher talked about both grandfather and grandmother. He noted that passing on stories in his American Indian community during his youth was done orally. They would gather around a campfire, and the eldest would talk, often it was the grandmother.

Listening:
- Reflect and write about how you describe or define your personal and family identity. Write about thoughts you have about your own ethnicity, neighborhood, spirituality, nationality, or language. What is important and not important to you about this aspect of yourself and why?
- Now write about your earliest memories of this part of yourself that you just wrote about. What was enjoyable or painful as you learned about these aspects of your identity?
- Many poets' work is about identity. A few are Francisco X. Alarcón, Gloria Anzaldúa, Lucille Clifton, Billy Collins, and Mary Kay Rummel. Choose a poet to read a few poems about identity.

Dialogue:
- With a partner, discuss your own family stories and these poems. What connections can you make between your stories and those of the poet?

Action:
- Read the following memory of one teacher education student:

> I vividly remember my uncle reading me a bedtime story every night while I was visiting him in Slovakia and I would listen intently to every work and watch his facial expressions and imagine all the fantastic magical worlds he would describe. I looked forward to that every night. My mom would sometimes make up stories but only occasionally. But when she did, they were better than any story that was ever read because they were especially fantastical and imaginative and original and of course because they were from mommy.

This same student, in a discussion about second language acquisition, remarked that she was surprised to learn of the research that said that a child should be taught in her native language in school, while also studying English, so that language could develop fully in both languages. She explained that her family had spoken Slovak at home and when she went to school at age 5, English was the language of instruction. She loved school, loved English and was very successful in school.

After reading her above journal response, do you have any idea why this student as a child was able to transition into English learning with such ease? In what ways was her family supporting her home language development?

- Interview a relative or friend about some of your memories that you have been writing about. Interview another acquaintance from a different background from your own. Write a short report, write a poem, write a skit, or paint a picture about the similarities and differences of the family memories.

- Read *Immigrant Learners and Their Families* by Weinstein-Shr and Quintero (1994, Delta Systems) and *The Middle of Everywhere* by Pipher (2002), which documents refugee and immigrant families' experiences. Identify educational programs and supports which use family strengths and realistically provide services to the families. Plan a way to collect data in your community to learn the strengths and needs of refugee and immigrant families. Compile a list of all existing programs which may provide support. Evaluate whether or not the programs existing actually meet the needs of the families.

- Choose a Web site and investigate information about families in your choice of interest areas:

It's Elementary: Talking About Gay Issues in School
http://www.womedia.org/our/elem.html

Single Parents
http://singleparentsnetwork.com

Teen Parents
http://www.pamf.org/teen/parents.cfm

Grandparents Raising Children
http://www.aarp.org/confacts/programs/grandraising.html

Step Parents
http://www.geocities.com/stepmomx3/

- Choose one of the following readings or another you may find that addresses issues of families, their strengths and their barriers:

Blackledge, A. (March, 1999). Language literacy and social justice: The experiences of Bangladeshi women in Birmingham, UK. *Journal of Multilingual and Multicultural Development, 20*, pp. 170–103.
Polakow, V. (1993). *Lives on the edge*. Chicago, IL: University of Chicago Press.
Quintanilla, R. (1997). Raul Quintanilla. In Rummel, M. & Quintero, E. *Teachers' reading/Teachers' lives*. Albany, NY: SUNY Press.
Quintero, E. (2004). Will I lose a tooth? Will I learn to Read? *Young Children*. Washington, DC: NAEYC.
Swadener, B. & Kessler, S. (1995). *Children and families "At Promise": Deconstructing the discourse of risk*. Albany, NY: SUNY Press.

Excerpts from University Student Responses

After going through a series of similar activities relating to family history, a group of students wrote reflections in their journals. A few excerpts are:

> I'm Chinese-American and in the Chinese community, I would be described as a jook-sing, in other words, a child born in America that has adopted many American customs and characteristics. Being Chinese was not something I was proud of when I was younger and because of that I failed to learn as much of the language as I could have, which I feel is a big part of being Chinese. - Through this language I am able to have conversations with people who can fill me in on what being Chinese is all about. But because my ability is limited I am often shy with my relatives who only speak Chinese. I don't want to be branded a jook-sing although I feel I am one. I am proud to be Chinese but when people ask me to tell them details about Chinese culture I'm afraid that I may fall short in explaining the complexity of it all. This aspect of me is important; it connects me to my family and their values. I am the way I am because of my ethnicity. I have accepted some of these beliefs and values as my own but I have also rebelled against some values that clash with my understanding of the world. I feel the latter aspect of myself can be attributed to my Americanized side.
>
> I don't tie my ethnicity to a particular place. I bring it wherever I go. However, I will say this, I feel my Chinese-ness the most if I am the only Chinese person in a particular place. I rarely feel this way in New York because of its diversity. Mostly I carry both plates in my hands wherever I go but the people and the place will determine which one will be heavier.

> When I think of my ethnic identity, honestly I think of so many things I don't know where to start. My family come from all over the place actually, so I don't really know which ethnic group I identify myself with most. My mother is American by birth, as is her mother. But, my grandmother grew up in Mexico, as did my grandfather. My grandmother's family was from Mexico. My grandfather's father was from Greece, his mother from Mexico. My father, born in Mexico, is of European descent. His father was born in Stockholm, his mother in San Antonio, right next to the Alamo. My grandmother also has Swedish and German ancestry. And while he is not Latino, my father grew up in Venezuela. These are all of the things I think of when I think of my ethnic background. I tend to relate more to the Hispanic side of my family, because I grew up in San Antonio where there is such a large Hispanic population. I guess that would be the place my ethnic identity is tied to. Everyone in my family speaks Spanish; all my grandparents, aunts, uncles, etc. While the history of Mexican people has not played a large role in my upbringing, I know

some of it, mostly what I learned in school and from my surroundings. People in San Antonio are very aware of the Mexican culture and this is shown in various ways throughout the city. Even though I am American, I relate to the Mexican culture most out of all of my backgrounds because it plays such a vital role in my everyday life. There is not a large Swedish or Greek community in San Antonio. The earliest things I remember about my cultural background and ethnicity are the traditions of my family. I did not know much about Swedish people, but I knew what they ate at Christmas time. I knew some of their manners from stories told to me by my father's parents. I knew about the Greeks and what kinds of things they did at Easter. My mother's parents would take us to the Greek Festival held each year at St. Sophia's Greek Orthodox Church downtown. This is how I was introduced to my ethnic background.

When I think of race and ethnicity, I realize how complex of an issue it is. Because of my background, I look white to most people who meet me. Many people are surprised to learn that I am Hispanic. While many Hispanics that I know have encountered racism before, I have not because I do not appear to be Hispanic. I have a hard time saying that I am either white or Hispanic. Both ethnicities are part of me, so I cannot say which I identify with more.

I hope this all makes sense to you. It seems like it all fits in my head. When I have thought about it before, I never thought I was confused about this. It seems like I am a bit, though. I think part of it is what I have learned about race and ethnicity and culture over the past few years. They are not things that are so easily defined, I guess.

So What Can Educators Do to Support Multicultural Child-rearing and Learning?

Educators around the world have been facing stark challenges that seem to only become more complex as the months proceed. On the one hand, all over the Middle East, the Balkans, and into Africa, successive generations have handed down a legacy of loss, desperation, and betrayal to their offspring. The political and economic conditions affect all aspects of education. On the other hand, economic globalization—with all its disadvantages and advantages—has uprooted families and brought people together in previously unpredictable circumstances.

At a teacher development seminar for Head Start teachers with multicultural, multilingual programs in Minnesota, issues were addressed about making the early learning curriculum responsive to children's real lives, their strengths, and needs. There was much discussion and many suggestions were made in the groups about activities supporting Hmong, Lao, and Vietnamese children because those refugee groups had been in Minnesota for a number of years. Trust had been developed between the families and the programs, many of the parents had learned enough English to be able to assist the staff in curriculum development. Furthermore, storybooks and historical accounts of these groups had recently become available to educators.

Then the refugees began arriving from Somalia. The teachers and staff talked about the numbers of vibrant, curious children and their respectful and quiet parents. The refugees came from a terrible war-torn reality and few had more than two or three words of English. One Head Start teacher stood up and said, "I have a story about what I learned from the Somali children about curriculum."

She explained that in her class of twenty three- and four-year-olds that year, twelve were children recently from Somalia. She related her attempts to gain the trust of the children, to include them in the regular activities of the program, and to talk with the mothers when they brought the children to school. She said that through gestures and human non-verbal kindness, she thought the children were feeling safe. But they seldom played with children other than those from their group of Somali friends and seemed to be picking up very little English so other than through observing them, she couldn't find out about their family stories, their interests, or their needs. She tried to ask for help from the mothers, but the language barrier prevented almost any communication.

One Sunday evening, in desperation of thinking about what she was going to provide for the children on Monday, she took a large garbage bag and went to her own children and her neighbors' children to ask for donations of stuffed animal toys. The next morning, she entered the classroom and after greeting the children, she dumped the contents of the bag on the rug in the middle of the room.

There happened to be a stuffed camel among the animals, and the Somali kids jumped on it and started talking animatedly about the animal. Some went immediately to the sand table and started making what seemed to be a desert scene with dunes and troughs for water for animals and tents for the tiny plastic "people." Some other children went immediately to the art center and began drawing camels and their own versions of camel activities. Others went to the house center and began using the props available to prepare for some sort of feast.

The teacher was thrilled and immediately was able to ascertain from the children, with small bits of information from the mothers, that camels had been an integral part of these families' lives. They used camels for transportation, they raised them carefully and of course, became very attached to their family animals as American children do to house pets. They used the products of the camel for cooking and other life-maintaining needs. A study of camels, the teacher reported, ensued for at least six weeks. The events were important for the Somali children in that they could become the "experts" and teach the teachers and other children. In this teaching they began to learn and use more English (and Spanish) in order to get their messages across. The information also was invaluable to the other children and the staff.

Dr. Winsome Gordon of UNESCO, spoke at an international Early Childhood Education conference in March, 2002. She told of countless school visits to schools in many African and Asian countries. She spoke of the six and seven-year-old children coming to school with much real world knowledge and then being handed a watered-down, inappropriate curriculum that treats them as immature innocents. She called for early years educators to acknowledge the experiences these students come to school with. Maybe it is the experience of caring for younger and elder family members, the experience of daily shopping and negotiating the family's food supply, the experience of cooperative survival in a refugee camp, the experience of survival during or cleaning up after war. While these students, of course, need the knowledge and skills taught in school curricula, their "funds of knowledge" (Moll, 1992) must be recognized and built upon. To begin to understand a culture, teachers must study the folk tales, legends, history, and current culture of a group of people. It is not adequate to study only the ancestry of a culture and ignore how that culture has evolved and changed through the ages. Children need the opportunity to react to multicultural ideas through a variety of activities such as drawing, journal writing, and storytelling. Multicultural curriculum utilizes literacy events to strengthen children's understanding of various cultures and people. These literacy events can only be carried out when cultures have been researched by the children's teacher.

Listening:
- Write in your journal about some things you believe are wonderful about your family. Now, write a little about if there is anything you wish were different about your family. Does this characteristic embarrass you or annoy you? Why?
- Read *Halmoni and the Picnic* by Sook Nui Choy

Dialogue:
- What did you learn about Halmoni's family? Who are the characters? What obstacles were they challenged with?
- Discuss any ways your family stories relate to Halmoni's.

Action:
- Interview a classmate or an acquaintance whose parent or relative didn't speak the language of the neighborhood or school during that person's childhood. What things embarrassed the child? How did the child cope with the difficulty? Who helped? Report to the class and then make some suggestions about how schools and teachers can be more supportive.

Listening:
- Write about an experience in which you didn't "fit in." Did you feel isolated because of people, laws, customs, or all of the above? Write about borders, immigration, law, colonization, oppression, transformation and pluralism.
- Read *Friends from the Other Side: Amigos del Otro Lado* by Gloria Anzaldúa.

Dialogue:
- Discuss with a small group the strengths and barriers of the characters. Discuss any connections you can make between the story and the experiences you wrote about above.

Action:
- Read the following facts relayed by an activist speaker (Wise, 1998) and choose one to relate to other information discussed in this chapter. Prepare a report for your group.

  1. Power and access to resources by 2030 in the United States one half of all the people in the workforce will be people of color and over half the students will be from families of color.
  2. Equity is the more important word (than diversity).
  3. You are responsible for 10,000 dead bodies per year of poor people of color because of inadequate health care.
  4. In Minnesota a survey from *The Star Tribune* two-thirds of whites in suburbs said it would be a good idea to bus white kids from the suburbs to inner city for school. The next question was would you send your children to the inner city for school and only 7% said yes.

- Now write a short essay about how this storybook and this small collection of facts affects you as a teacher.
- Investigate one of the following readings (or, of course, a related one that you know about but haven't had time to read) and report to your class.

Commeyras, M., Sullivan, A.M. and Montsi, M. with Bontshetse Mazile, Ilke Dunne, Bontle Menyatso, Thala Montsi, Doreen Yorke (2003) Nothing Else But to Be a Woman: The Poetics of Gender in Southern Africa, in E. Quintero & M. Rummel, *Becoming a teacher in the new society: Bringing communities and classrooms together.* New York: Peter Lang.

Shigaki, I. S. (1987). Language and the transmission of values: Implications from Japanese Day Care. In B. Fillion, C. Hedley, & E. DiMartino (Eds.), *Home and school: Early language and reading.* Norwood, N. J.: Ablex Publ. Corp.

Swadener, Beth B. (2002). *Does the village still raise the child?: A collaborative study of changing child-rearing and early education in Kenya.* Albany, NY: SUNY Press.

Tobin, J. (1995). *Preschool in three cultures.* New York: Teachers College Press.

- Choose one of the following Web sites to investigate and report on your information as it relates to previous discussions and activities:

Resource Center of the Americas
http://www.americas.org/

Early Childhood Education in China by JoAnn Vaughan
http://www.pbs.org/kcts/preciouschildren/earlyed/read_vaughan.html

- Write about an experience in which you were unable to understand the language in which someone was attempting to communicate with you. Maybe the language was a different language from one you understand, or maybe the dialect was unfamiliar to you, or maybe the terms used were simply unknown to you.
- Read the following journal entry from a graduate student who had the writing assignment about being in a situation in which language and communication was an issue:

My most recent experience with trying to communicate with someone who speaks another language was last Friday when I took the Chinatown to Chinatown bus from New York to DC. Immediately after exiting my taxi two women approached me and began shouting, yes-shouting, "DC! DC!" I gathered they wanted to know if I wanted to purchase a ticket to DC, but they did not question me and ask, "DC?" They simply shouted, "DC." I have taken this bus several times and knew that the price was $35 round trip, but when I pulled out my money one of the women said, "Thirty-four dollar." I was surprised, but thought perhaps they changed the price and handed over $34. She looked at me and stuck the money out and repeated, "Thirty-four dollar." I said, "Yes, thirty-four dollars. Here." She then held up one finger and I understood she really meant $35. I said, "You mean thirty-five dollars?" and she repeated, "Yeah, thirty-four dollar." It was a minor mistake, but it did annoy me. I was tired and in a rush and in no mood to be culturally sensitive. I just wanted my darn ticket! Getting a seat on this bus is always a major adventure as the system they have for selling and assigning seats is enforced only irregularly and depends on how many people complain. Initially, we are given seat assignments for the time of our scheduled bus, but since they often overbook because of multiple people selling tickets and not communicating with each other, people are frequently given tickets for the same seat or are bumped from previous buses. Heated arguments ALWAYS break out between passengers and between passengers and the management, none of whom speak English even close to conversationally. The bus is always late and one always runs the risk of getting kicked off or yelled at, but I keep going back because you can't beat the price. However, the experience always leaves a bad taste in my mouth. I joke about it with my Chinese friends and many of them have stated that they would never take this bus for exactly the reasons I explained and joke about "their people" not being so good at organizing transportation and sticking to schedules. I know that the people who run the buses are not less intelligent than me or most Americans, but when I see this kind of madness and poor planning, I can't help but question not only their business skills, but their intelligence too. To be clear, this is a fleeting thought that pops up in the heat of the moment, but it nevertheless is there. I'm only being honest.

Most of my closest friends are Asian of various backgrounds—Chinese, Vietnamese, Thai, Japanese, Korean, etc—and I think I am generally aware of many of the differences in communication and culture. Being aware makes me more understanding than some other people I imagine, but I still can't help getting frustrated and impatient when communication breaks down. In speaking with my friends, I've learned how in some cultures, such as Chinese or Vietnamese, being blunt or rushing people along is not a sign of rudeness and is simply a norm and style of interacting; however, in some other cultures, such as Japanese, choosing one's words carefully so that they always send a clear message of respect and patience is important. I think it would be wonderful to be fluent in another language because, among many other reasons, I would be able to see how words are used differently to convey particular messages. It would also be fascinating to learn which words do not have direct translations into English and therefore indicate an idea or thing that English-speakers have no concept of. What does the chaos of my Chinese bus traveling experience tell me about Chinese culture? Does it reflect their more communal approach to life-

evidenced by their obvious contrast to predictable schedules and rules? Is this seen in the language? How?

Learning from Families in Difficult Situations

Because my colleagues and I believe that we teachers must make an effort to learn from families in a variety of situations, we have begun qualitative research in Central America and Turkey has further emphasized the cultural and political and historical effect a family situation has on children. The participants are Iranian and Iraqi refugee women in Ankara, Turkey and the other groups of mothers in Guatemala. The interviews are framed by the following questions: In what ways are caregivers able to educate (talk to, read to, tell stories to, or sing with) your children within the context of refugee camps or other refugee contexts? How do you give important learning information to your children, through stories or activities? Are programs available to support the children's learning where you live now? The interview data was categorized and analyzed according to the theoretical perspectives framing the study and then selections are used in the problem-posing lessons for the university students.

The information gleaned from the interviews with the refugees informed both educators and policymakers about the strengths and needs of refugee women and children in terms of critical literacy and learning. This information could be used around the world in creating pedagogy for literacy, using local knowledge of particular sites and drawing on a range of strengths and histories for families and children to advocate for their rights to literacy and learning in difficult times.

In the summer of 2002, a colleague at Middle Eastern Technical University in Ankara, Turkey and I began interviewing refugee mothers. We were interested in documenting parents' strengths and challenges. We found that those fifteen interviews just barely touched on what are grave and dramatic worldwide problems for refugees and their children. We were struck by the severity of the needs and the lack of information both for the refugees themselves and the agencies and educational institutions which may be in a position to ultimately provide some assistance when the refugees resettle.

We interviewed the Director of the Turkish Office of United Nations Higher Commission on Refugees. We learned that the 1951 Geneva Convention dictates that refugees can be in Turkey temporarily as asylum seekers; and that they must apply to be recognized as refugees in order to receive services.

On average, the refugees register within 10 days of being in the country (Turkey). There are three steps to process: First there is an interview, and then the refugee must wait two to three months for a decision. The second phase is a waiting period for resettlement in U.S., Canada, Australia, and Scandinavian countries and other countries which accept refugees. The average total time for resettlement is one to two years. There is an appeal process when refugee status is denied. There is a limit to the number who can be asylum seekers. Some estimates of refugees granted and denied asylum status indicate that only one in ten of refugees who apply for asylum status are granted the status (Icduygu, 2000). If asylum status is granted, the refugees have financial, medical, social and psychological counseling. If asylum status is not granted, the refugees receive nothing. No money, no medical assistance, no schooling, no work permits. Nothing.

In a literacy course for teacher education masters students, some of the information was presented and used with other course content. The course goals were to survey literary genres and literacy materials, to explore the manner in which culture is reflected in and influences literary genres and literacy materials, to explore the relationship of critical literacy to the political, social and historical strengths tensions and funds of local knowledge of various social groups. The class was introduced to problem-posing pedagogy. Each week the class periods were structured in a problem-posing format.

After a few weeks' investigation into the politics and pedagogical issues of literacy programs for bilingual, multilingual students who are learning English in schools, the students were asked to synthesize that information with the complexities of supporting the literacy education of refugee students.

I explained to the teacher education students about the research my colleagues and I are involved in collecting interviews from women in refugee situations in Central America and the Middle East. We had the special experience of a guest visit of the colleague who had collected interviews in Guatemala. We began the problem-posing activities that evening with information in poetry format that had been developed from the actual interview texts from Guatemala.

What Mothers Do

Listening:
- Think and write about a mother figure in your life or your own mothering. What support did that person need from the community in order to mother? From the schools? From the government?

- Remember one strong experience related to mothering. What is some important thing that a mother figure did for you? What did that person do or make? Try to hear that person talking to you. What are some things that person says (or said). Write it down.
- Read the following poem.

What Mothers Do
Mary Kay Rummel

Call her not Noemi that is beautiful
But Mara that is bitter
For the Almighty hath quite
filled her with bitterness . . . Catholic liturgy for
stations of the cross
In Guatemala red is Mary's color
At the side altar in La Iglesia de San Francisco
the Mayan Mary is a shepherdess with long curled hair
skin darkened by sun and time surrounded by three lambs.
Today her gown is plain red velvet, her straw hat embroidered
with bright flowers, the shepherdess before the sorrow,
before the child, and after when he is feeding
from her breast.
In front of her we chant
"Lamb, Lamb, Lamb"
I walk the cobbled courtyard outside the church
under the spell of Naomi, find her and Mara both
in a young girl who sits and weaves, loom in lap
her finished tapetes arranged carefully behind her.
Her blouse is blue embroidered with flowers
her arms strong with the push and pull of thread.
She fast talks with silences between words that I
can't hear to her son who sits on a basket
across from her, his brown eyes lost in the distance
or sometimes turned down as he is wound in her words.
She talks in the rhythm of the weave—her voice rising
with teaching, praying, complaining, working
the skeins of her words, the world she is.
Lamb, we chant to her,
Lamb, Lamb, Lamb

La Antigua, Guatemala

Dialogue:
- What work is the mother in this poem doing? What could she be saying to her child as she works? What is she teaching? How is she keeping her child near?
- Discuss choices you make in your daily life that take a stand.
- Brainstorm with your group ways the different choices we all make influence teaching and learning.

Action:
- Go to the Web site for The Resource Center of the Americas, http://www.americas.org/. This is a Minneapolis-based nonprofit publisher of AMERICAS.ORG which is devoted to the notion that every person in this world is entitled to the same fundamental human rights. Their starting point for promoting these rights is learning and teaching about the peoples and countries of the Americas—their history, culture and politics. Read one or more of the articles and relate the information to the poem.
- From your reading at the Web site, describe the ways the women of Guatemala have organized to sell their weaving. Read the article about Colibri and the organizing of Guatemalan weavers.
- Read the poem

A Dozen Reasons to Give Up Haggling
Over the Price of Weavings
Rosanne Lloyd
(www.CyberPoet.com/RoseannLloyd.html)

1 For the weaver herself who takes the bus to market at 4 a.m.
1.5 for the buck and a half she brings home each day
2 for the discount rate *para dos* she offers too readily
3 for the 3 languages she speaks, working on the 4th
4 for her babies born after the war
one for the cousin killed in the highlands
one for uncle in Minnesota
two for the brother and sister hiding in Mexico
5 for the age she started to weave
6 for her favorite colors: canario, rojo, verde, morado, indigo y cafe
7 for the quetzal/dollar exchange
8 for the animals that dance in her cloth: cat, quetzal, monarchs, deer,
  baby chickens, dog, squirrel eating chamomile, dove

9 for the tortillas in her apron pocket
10 for ten fingers she says she's lucky to have
11 for the family she has to feed
12 for the men, the dozens of unmarked graves

- Write a poem based on this model, "A Dozen Reasons to . . ." Think about issues you could have your students write about related to the topic of taking a stand as educators. (I.e. A dozen reasons to have children use their home language . . .)
- Share ideas for applying problem posing to your teaching.

Then the same students were introduced to *Refugee Knowledge: Learning from Refugee Mothers*

Listening:
- Read more of the introduction to the refugee interview research report:

In August of 2002, all of our interview informants had been denied asylum status. The first woman we interviewed, whose husband had been a police officer in Iran and then because of refusal to carry out an "unethical and inhuman" procedure, he and his family were driven from Iran at gunpoint. The family applied for asylum status and was denied. We asked the interviewee if they were told why they were denied, "No. Not even when I tried to find out, they wouldn't talk to me. They said my file was closed."

Still this woman does her best to help to educate her own two children and those young children of other refugees in the same situation. She said:

I borrow books (in Farsi) that some other refugees have or have made for the children. I use the books so that they don't forget their culture and language. It is important to have contact with other refugees. . .

Her children are not permitted to go to school. Because they fear for their safety, they cannot return to their country.

Another woman we interviewed explained that her family has been in Turkey for four years. She has three children, twin boys and a daughter. They were rejected for asylum status by United Nations Higher Commission on Refugees, so she slept in front of their office door for forty days and nights to learn why they were rejected and to protest their decision. She was never told. She explained:

We are political refugees. My two brothers were sentenced to death and killed. They were members of Halkın Mücahitleri which is an opposition organization. My other brother ran away from Iran without a passport.

We are not members of that organization, but because of my brothers the government always bothered us. My kids could not go to school freely. Then we had to run away from the country to be safe. . . . My sons forgot their mother tongue. I can not teach them because my stress level is very high. I also have to work because my husband is sick and he cannot work.

We interviewed another family. The mother did not speak English or Turkish, so her husband talked with us. They are from Iraq. They have four children, ages 7, 9, 12, 14. They have been here in Turkey for eighteen months. The United Nations Higher Commission on Refugees denied him assylum status and closed his family's case. He can not find a job because people did not want somebody who does not have an identity authorized by Turkish Government. At the same time they don't have anybody who can be a guide for them to find an illegal job. The church pays their rent and gives them eighteen dollars for food every two weeks. They can only buy bread with that money. The father said he tries to teach the children English. He said, "There is no play, no pictures, no picnics . . . nothing for my children." The only activity they engage in is coming to church, but sometimes they can not come because they don't have money to give the dolmu (bus). Sometimes they have to walk a long way. When we asked what were his hopes for his children in the future, he said, " To have a country." He went into detail about his reasons for being a refugee.

I could not betray my conscience and become a spy working for the Iraqi regime. All my problems were due to the simple fact that I did not deceive and surrender three persons working for the United Nations Oil-for-Food programme as inspectors to the Iraqi intelligence on espionage over Iraq. My torturers told me that they would be accused of espionage working for the Americans against Saddam. Every Iraqi working for the projects under Oil-for-Food programme has been expected to report on internaitonal staff back to Bagdad. As I refused to collaborate in that, I was being accused of espionage as well and I was severely subjected to torture and ill treatment by the Muhabarat. (He and his wife were both assaulted and thugs broke the arm of his seven-year-old son. When agents showed him his death warrant signed by Hussein, he and his wife and children fled.) I had been working for the United Nations under contract for four and a half years, I had a very good life, house, a shop, a car. I had to leave all that and flee to Turkey seeking asylum.

- Read additional information from interview transcripts. (Each small group read about one family.)

Dialogue:
- Please discuss what was new information for you here. Please discuss ways you, as a Literacy Specialist in an Elementary, Middle, or High School may

support these students and their families if they arrived at your school tomorrow. How might you help the other teachers and educational community support the students?

Action:
- Now in small groups, please put some of the above requested "plans for support" in writing.

Excerpts from Student Responses

Group 1

This was a difficult assignment, even with help from Elena and Amy. From the description of Habib's four children and their lack of peer socialization for the past 18 months, I would ask the elementary school teachers to prepare their students for the new addition to their classroom. In order to build empathy, the teacher can lead students in a discussion of how they would feel if they were coming to a new school in a different country where the language is different. This discussion can lead into the topic of, things we all can do to make this new student feel welcome. The middle school teachers can ask for a volunteer, someone who will show the new student around and be a guiding shadow. I think the buddy system will also work for the elementary classrooms as well

Since three of the oldest children have been in school before and are literate in their own language, this will make the language transfer easier. I think that's true from what I've read about bilingual education. However, since the children picked up Turkish just from watching TV and not from any interactions, it seems that with the social interaction they should pick the language up in due time. In order to facilitate the language learning, I think a pull out teacher would be a good idea so that these four children can get individual attention. In order to motivate and connect with the students, their interests should be incorporated into their learning. High interest books should be easily accessible as well as books that have pictures supporting the text.

Group 2

For Leila's son, who is seventeen, one of my main concerns would be to provide him with materials that will not make him feel like we are babying him. Even though he is seventeen, he hasn't been in school since he was 14 so he will be lacking the skills most high school students have, and when you add that he does not speak English, it will be even harder to find texts for him that will not belittle him. I would try to use what I know about his interests, such as airplanes, and find texts about flying. Maybe we could start out with texts that he composes with the teacher so that he feels a sense of ownership with them. Since he has no background with English, teaching sounds is going to be necessary, but since he already has the knowledge of how language and reading work, it will not need to be as simplistic as what we teach kindergarten students. I would emphasize that skills be taught in context and through subjects that are relevant to him and to his culture. For Leila's daughter, who is thirteen, I would probably want to make sure that she feels welcome in the school. I might pair her up with a student from her class that can show her around and introduce her to people. Since she already has started learning English on her own, I know that she is motivated to learn the language, so interaction with other students will help her continue to learn English. She has trouble finding books so I would be sure to direct her to books that would be at her level. Since she is such an intelligent girl, I would have to make sure they were high-interest, but low-level books so that she could gradually work up to more difficult texts, and still have interesting, engaging texts to read.

I would want to make sure that both students felt comfortable in their new classes, so I would suggest preparing the classes for their arrival. I think it would be helpful for the classes to know where these students are coming from. They might want to read about their country and maybe think of questions they could ask the students when they arrived. Also, it would be extremely helpful for the teachers to know about the political situation of the country so that they would be aware of what these students had experienced before coming here. I would also find someone in the community who could help us communicate with the parents of these students. It is important for the parents to feel that their culture is valued by the school.

Group 3

I will be writing about Azime's family. Azime has a daughter, 13, and twin sons, 11. Most importantly for all of the refugee students, we thought the teachers need to create a warm, welcoming environment. S/he could do this by informing the children of the children coming and giving them a little of their background. We also thought that the teacher should assign one or two dependable students to each new student to help them get established in the school and classroom. We figured since the daughter loves to study and read and taught herself how to speak English and Turkish, that she could meet with her brothers (and other refugee students in the school) to offer support and guidance. The teachers should find out what the boys are interested in then find high interest, low skill books to help them develop beginning reading skills. We thought since the two boys fight a lot and have never been to school that their social skills would be at risk. In this case, the classroom community may be very overwhelming to them. The teacher should facilitate many small group activities and support these students through them. Conflict/resolution and self-esteem activities would also be helpful. Also, since these particular students would be coming in with little or no English skills, the teacher needs to find material in their native language and make sure everything is labeled in the room.

Implications

So, we have these many varied, strong, and committed parents from a multitude of backgrounds becoming a part of our school communities. What do we do? Vicki Braithwaite in New York City (1998) has some ideas:

> We could sponsor events once a month where we would invite parents, teachers, administrators, out to see and hear discussions. In my role now, we give workshops at school where we invite parents in and encourage teachers to staff development.
>
> Invite parents to come in to the classroom. Have that baby come in and let the kids be little scientists, researchers. When does the baby first crawl? Watching it crawl, jotting information down. Maybe the parent brings baby in two months later. Baby is now standing up. Children note this information. When is moment of baby's first words? Children interview mother, so they're learning sensitivity on how to care for another human being. What it is like to have a sibling in the home.
>
> Parents are so important. We ask teachers to be creative, they want to learn. Lots of times they have phobias about schools themselves. They don't know or aren't sure about their own literacy so don't want to be discovered if it isn't so strong. You have to tap into creativity resources there. Lots of times it is not in very formal ways. That could be something like masters of hairstyles, learn about culture, meaning of hairstyles. Using parents' strengths that are not so much pencil and paper, but other ways.

References

Alarcón, Francisco X. (1997). *Laughing tomatoes/Jitomates risueños.* San Francisco, CA. Children's Book Press.

Allen, Paula G. (1992). *Grandmothers of the light.* Boston: Beacon.

Anzaldúa, G. (1993). *Friends from the other side: Amigos del otro lado.* San Francisco, CA. Children's Book Press.

Ashton Warner, S. (1963). *Teacher.* New York: Simon & Schuster Trade Paperbacks.

Brathwaite, V. (1999). New York: Personal Conversation.

Choy, Sook N. (1993). *Halmoni and the picnic.* New York: Houghton Miflin.

Choy, Sook N. (1991). *The year of impossible good-byes.* New York: Dell Publishing.

Hoffman, M. (1995). *Boundless Grace.* New York: Penguin Group.

Moll, L. (1994). Funds of knowledge: A look at Luis Moll's research into hidden family resources. *CITYSCHOOLS, 1*(1), 19–21.

Rummel, M. K. & Quintero, E. P. (1997). *Teachers' reading/teachers' lives.* Albany, NY: SUNY Press.

Walker, A. (1990). *The color purple.* New York: Pocket Books.

Wise, T. (1998). Lecture at University of Minnesota Duluth. Duluth, MN.

·4·

INTEGRATING CURRICULUM FOR BIRTH–TODDLER AGE GROUP

*On the day you were born a circle of people welcomed you
with voices familiar and clear.*
FRASIER, 1997

It is important to understand that even very young children have begun a quest for identity. As Derman-Sparks (1992) points out, children are not "blank slates" when it comes to diversity nor are they color blind. They have already been exposed to social biases and people's identities. Most importantly "between 2½ and 3½ years of age, children also become aware of and begin absorbing socially prevailing negative stereotypes, feelings, and ideas about people based on gender, race, ethnicity, class, and disabilities" (Derman-Sparks, 1992, p. 117). All children are aware of differences and family lifestyles. Researchers "argue for the integration of a multicultural perspective into all aspects of the environment and for curriculum that uses research about the development of identity and attitudes and incorporates basic principles of sound early childhood education" (Derman-Sparks, 1992, p. 116).

This chapter will explore ways to use children's literature in problem-posing format to support an integrated curriculum for infants and toddlers. As previously stated, we have interpreted "multicultural" in terms of the literature we have used in a very broad sense. We stress the importance of using literature, stories, folk tales and legends from cultures that have previously been silenced through censorship, politics, or simply from lack of information. We also believe it is important to use appropriate, good literature from the United States and Western Europe too. What toddler doesn't enjoy Dr. Seuss?

Through this method, it is possible to investigate the development of infants and toddlers and to think about and plan for designing healthy, supportive environments for infants and toddlers. Current events and environments in which the children live and how those contexts affect the children can also be addressed using this method.

Growth and Development Through Many Lenses

The most exciting aspect of being an early childhood professional is that you have the opportunity to observe and support the growth of young children. While we explore ways to use literature with young children, it is important to always keep in mind our necessity to observe children's development in their contexts of community, home, and school. It is important to remember that each child is a developing individual, affected by and affecting her family and community. In other words, social, cultural, and economic factors have immense influence on child development. As early childhood professionals it is our responsibility to continue to study the changing factors in the world today because we all are affected by them. Lubeck (1994) reminds us,

> For years, the question of research has been how to best understand patterns of development in order to improve teaching, teacher education, and childhood while most current research does challenge to idea of child development through ideas that examine "development-in-context" (New, 1994) or the social, cultural, and economic factors that influence development. (p. 123)

It is also important to consider children's dispositions. A disposition is a tendency to exhibit frequently, consciously, and voluntarily a pattern of behavior that is directed to a broad goal (Katz, 1993). Another way of referring to a person's disposition is her temperament. Katz (1993) stresses the importance of paying attention to dispositions because ". . . the acquisition of knowledge and skills does not guarantee that they will be used and applied (p. 47). Thus, it is important that a child learn knowledge and skills while having the disposition to use the knowledge and skills strengthened. "For the moment, one of the most important dispositions to be listed in educational goals is the disposition to go on learning" (Katz, 1993, p. 47).

Educators have been studying children's development since the early 1900s. At that time, the child study movement focused on the characteristics of young children at each age and the influence of heredity and environment. The information we have today about child development comes from a wide variety of sources. Today's knowledge comes from studies in sociology, psychology, linguistics, medicine, health, anthropology, history, and education. This serves as a reminder of how important it is to be constantly watching children to learn about their development. We must observe with respect the family and community raising the child and make no assumptions based upon our own limited knowledge of their worlds.

Beth Blue Swadener (2000) and her Kenyan collaborators show us many issues to consider regarding early childhood and community in a country whose environments and national policies are relatively unknown to American educators. In addition to informing ourselves about a culture and a country's social policy, we also read in *Does the Village Still Raise the Child: A Collaborative Study of Changing Child-rearing and Early Education in Kenya* about many issues very pertinent to the field here in the United States.

Listening:
- Write a few personal notes about conversations in your family which you remember. In particular, think about a young child or toddler's childhood speech. The child may be you or a family member or friend. What were the child's first words, childhood speech, and/or developmental highlights (funny, fast, slow, different, same . . .) Write about discussions about family members' similarities and differences in terms of development and personality or temperament.
- Listen to or read *Leo the Late Bloomer* by Robert Kraus.

Dialogue:
- Please discuss: Did the story remind you of anything you just wrote about? Did it remind you of any children in the early childhood programs you interact with or observe in?

Action:
- Read the following principles of development. Many of the principles of development refer to development as learning, so I will use those words interchangeable. The descriptions have been developed from years of observations by early childhood educators who have extensive experiences and expertise. Even with the constantly changing body of knowledge about child development, there is some agreement (Driscoll & Nigell, 2000) about a few principles that help explain how children develop. Also, remember Freire's (1985) advice about problematizing ". . . involves a constant clarification of that which remains hidden within us while we move about in the world, though we are not necessarily regarding the world as the object of our critical reflection" (Freire, 1985, p. 107).

The Six Principles of Development

1. Individual variation is present in all areas of development and learning. This principle is the foundation of any theory of development. Children have different experiences, have different genetic makeups, and they come from different home environments, and they will grow and learn at different rates and in different ways.

2. In most cultures, development occurs in a somewhat predictable sequence, but the sequence varies from culture to culture. The word predictable does not mean that children do not move through the sequence in individual ways.

3. Children learn and develop best when their needs are met. Those needs include physical and emotional needs as well as social needs. Maslow's hierarchy of needs reminds us that basic needs of food and shelter, as well as emotional safety and a sense of belonging, must be met before humans can begin to attain other needs. Unfortunately, we live in a world that does not always assure that those basic needs are being met for all children. Consequently, those of us in the early childhood profession must often take care of hunger, fears, and loneliness in children before we can begin to teach or facilitate development.

4. All children learn from interacting with other children and adults and with the environment. These interactions include physical interactions children have as they touch, explore, and experiment with the physical world around them. The social interactions children have as they watch, play, and as they gradually cooperate with others are key to development. The adults in a child's life and the child's peers are major contributors to development. All the toys and materials you see in a preschool or child care center contribute to each child's development as well.

5. Children learn from play. Children's play, sometimes called "work" by them, promotes development in all aspects of growth. Play is the best context for children's learning and development because it is open ended and free, children have control over it, it can be done alone or with others, it can even occur without any materials or equipment, and it can take place in many contexts. It is important to realize different cultural groups have different ideas about the importance of play and often define "play" in different ways.

6. Children construct their own knowledge.

(Adapted from Driscoll and Nagel, 2000)

- Go to the Web and find more information about children growing up in cultural, historical, and political contexts different from those in the United States. Document some questions you have about these six principles of development for children in those contexts. Which of these principles in unfamiliar to you?
- Read Swadener, Beth B. (2000). *Does the Village Still Raise the Child: A Collaborative Study of Changing Child-rearing and Early Education in Kenya*. Albany,

NY: SUNY Press. Relate what you learn to the information discussed in this chapter and report to your class.

Planning for Integrated Curriculum for Infants Using Children's Literature

Regarding infant development, many factors help us focus on the situation before, during, and after birth that directly influence how a child will develop. They include: family economics (resources, needs, and limits), family support systems, family health (physical, emotional, and social), community and dominant themes within, educational levels of family members, cultural background of family, family size, and family attitudes toward pregnancy, children, education.

Listening:
- Reflect and write about what you know about the family situation during your own prenatal and neonatal development.
- Please listen to or read *On the Day You Were Born*, by Debra Frasier.

Dialogue:
- First, discuss which parts of this story moved you as a listener.
- Now, discuss in your small groups ways you see that by reading this story with a young baby, you would be addressing the information presented in the previous few paragraphs about development.

Action:
- Read Edwards, Patricia A. & Franklin, S.H. (1999). *A Path to Follow: Learning to Listen to Parents*. Portsmouth, NH: Heinemann or other research by Dr. Edwards that you can access on the World Wide Web or in your library. Answer Dr. Edwards's question: Why is it necessary to learn about the "human side" of children and families? Edwards designed a model of the Social World of Children which shows a close connection between community, family, and children and their learning. Using such a model, document how your literacy plans encourage engagement of all aspects of the children's world.
- Read the following remembrance from a teacher education student:

When my parents decided they wanted to be parents they plunged into it full force! They decided to start reading to my identical twin sister and me before we were even born. I can imagine my mom sitting with a book rested on her pregnant tummy as she read children's books to us. If I learned nothing else, I probably got very accustomed to the sound of her voice. Even after we were born there must have been a significant period of time when before we began to understand anything she was saying (early infancy) I'm sure by the time we were of reading age it was an automatic activity for us.

What do you think about this? Do you have similar stories from family and friends? Collect some stories and share with your class.

- Research some of the work of Valerie Polokow. She has interviewed many women who are living in dire situations and struggle to raise their infants and toddlers. She also has documented many of the recent changes in the welfare laws at the national level that have put mothers and infants most at risk at even more risk. Report to your class.
- Go to the Web site or find any of the print sources for The Children's Defense Fund and document some of the statistics that show the unfortunate reality for many infants and toddlers. Relate what you learned to what has been discussed here and to your future work as an early childhood teacher.
- Using this story, *On the Day You Were Born*, as an inspiration, compile a resource of activities you could do with a young infant that encourages learning about family, the earth, the trees and flowers, the animals, the moon, stars, and wind. Share a minimum of three of your activities with your class and at least one with an infant. Document what happened and what you learned by the experience in a personal journal or learning log.

In the past, little was known about infants' capabilities but today, people are aware of infants' incredible abilities. From the moment of birth, they make physiological adjustments that begin with breathing, eating, and eliminating. They adjust from a very secure, warm, and sheltered environment within their mothers to one of varied stimuli, with less security, and different temperatures. For these reasons, the first four weeks, the neonatal period, is a critical period in infant development. By the end of the neonatal period, the infant displays a number of inborn movements called reflexes—such as breathing, rooting, sucking, and eye blinks—or primitive reflexes—such as grasping and the startle reflex (which occurs when a loud noise or sudden movement causes the arms to thrust out from the body).

An infant's physical development is marked by observable changes in weight and length as well as internal changes of the central nervous system, bones, and muscles. As the nervous system matures, the bones and muscles grow and become coordinated. Consequently, in the first year of life, physical development is focused on movement. These changes in the infant's ability to move and manipulate his environment have many implications for the kind of environment he needs, the appropriate play materials, and the types of activities from which he can learn and enjoy.

Listening:
- Read *My Many Colored Days* by Dr. Seuss (the board book, if available).

Dialogue:
- Research of young infants (one to four months of age) tells us that a baby exhibits some sense of size, color, and shape recognition of objects in the immediate environment and that the infant moves eyes from one object to another. Discuss what comes to mind in terms of what you believe is some of the most important information for us as educators to focus on about infant development. Why would this be a good storybook to read to a young infant? What other "play" materials would you provide for the infant and caregiver? What activities would you do with the infant?

Action:
- Share some of your idea suggestions that could be used in activities with infants that you discussed above.
- Using the information we have about vocalization and language (the infant imitates gestures that are modeled and looks in the direction of a sound source and connects sound and rhythms with movement by moving or jiggling in time to music, singing, or chanting) discuss what comes to mind in terms of what you believe are some implications for us as educators to focus on about language in infant development. Begin a collection of music activities for young infants. Choose an activity that you have tried with a young baby. Share the activity, including materials, with your class, and report on how the baby on how the baby responded.
- Research the topic of infant stimulation. How much stimulation is too much? What are the signs an infant uses to tell us? Report to your class.
- Go to your library or the World Wide Web and review information about contexts of infant development in other countries. What are ways infant stimulation occurs there? What are the cultural norms for this in those contexts? Document what you learn and report to your class or your study group.

Magda Gerber (1998) in her life-long work with infants internationally gives us guidance about how we can provide infants with environments that encourage development. She believes that the first ingredient for healthy development is respect. She maintains that we must observe the child, tune in to her and follow her lead. She says infants learn motor skills and coping skills best from their own inner resources. She says that the social, emotional, and language skills are learned best by caring adults' help. She stresses the important of talking and "listening" to the baby.

Mothers and caregivers from different cultures often have different ways to listen and to communicate with babies. Educators had much to learn when there was an influx of Hmong people from Laos and Cambodia to Minnesota. A child care center with many Hmong children was trying to improve the infant and toddler program by hiring more Hmong staff. The center believed in a language-rich environment and much personal one-to-one interaction between caregiver and baby. With Hmong staff, they got very little interaction. This situation provided a very real example of a conflict of style in relating to babies. What would be normal in Hmong society? Mothers strap their babies to them, and this is what happened at the center. They have constant bodily interaction, but not the interaction of talking common to what the care givers previously knew (Greenman, 1989).

Furthermore, currently, children are seen not simply as passing through a universal set of stages, but also as setting out on a unique cognitive journey that is guided by cultural practices (Case and Okamoto, 1996). This cognitive journey of course includes all aspects of learning. For example, numeracy is viewed as a cultural practice that builds on innate mechanisms for understanding quantities. The result is a conceptual structure for numeracy that reflects both universal and culture-sensitive characteristics (Okamoto et al. 1996).

Listening:
- Please read *Demi's Dragons and Fantastic Creatures*, by Demi, a book about magical Chinese dragons and creatures.

Dialogue:
- The symbols used in the art work are Chinese symbols of all that is good, such as peace, courage, and wisdom. Discuss with your group your personal reactions to art work and the messages of symbols provided by the traditional symbols.
- Discuss now if you personally felt uncomfortable with some of the dragon art work. Discuss your feelings about whether or not you feel an infant would be afraid of the drawings.

Action:
- Read Gonzalez-Mena, Janet (1996). *Multicultural Issues in Child Care*. Mountainview, CA: Mayfield Publishing or other work by Gonzalez-Mena that you can find on the World Wide Web or in your library. What are dif-

fering practices of child care and child-rearing that influence infants' worlds? After you learn some new important content about this topic, develop five specific examples of adaptations or changes you will make in your practice based on the information.

- Do a search in the library and collect a few illustrated children's books that are familiar to you. Analyze them for illustrations that might be considered frightening to a child who is not familiar with the story. Share what you find with your class.
- Research literature books with illustrations from cultures that are not familiar to you. Bring a few of these books to class to continue the discussion about culture, development, cognition.
- Plan a way to decorate a center or a section of the room of the infant environment according to the themes of one or more of the storybooks you've found.

Normal social and emotional development of infants is characterized by the beginnings of trust and attachment, an array of emotions, crying and other forms of communication, and the start of social cognition. Each of these developments has important implications for the adults who interact with infants. Trust is learned by infants when their care is nurturing and predictable. The youngest infant soon realizes if she can depend on being comforted when upset, or changed when wet, or fed when hungry. This is the beginning of trust. In addition to trusting adults, infants learn to trust themselves. They learn that they have the capacity to get what they need by communicating with others. For example, an infant soon realizes that when she cries, one of the parents or other adults will comfort her; thus begins the baby's awakened sense of her ability to get what she needs. Attachment is a complex kind of bonding and an emotional relationship between an infant and a significant adult (mother, father, or caregiver). The observable characteristics are mutual affection and the desire or need for proximity of each other. Emotionally healthy infants form attachments gradually during their first year

Listening:
- Please read *Mama Do You Love Me* by Barbara M. Joosse, illustrated by Barbara Lavallee.

Dialogue:
- The little girl in the story is clearly a toddler, but this story is a joy and comfort for older infants to hear. Why do you think this is so? Discuss how this relates to the research about infant attachment.

- In addition to the beautiful illustrations and examples that show us a glimpse of Native Alaskan life, why would this book be useful and instructive to older infants and young toddlers?

Action:
- Do a search, both electronic and in the library, for storybooks that have the theme of a family's love for young children. Bring your findings to class.
- Participate in a demonstration fair of "Love Me" storybooks. Document the experience and the contributions by field notes, film, and photographs.
- Develop a brief plan for equipping all the centers in the early childhood environment (dramatic play area, a block center, a book center, a manipulative toy area, a large motor rumpus area, a science area, a sand and water table, and the art area) with a "Love Me" theme and that reflects the culture of the children in your field placement classroom.

Planning for Integrated Curriculum for Toddlers Using Children's Literature

It is difficult to say when infancy stops and toddlerhood begins; in fact, it is different for every child, which is why it is often given a range of 12 to 24 months. This is a very exciting time to observe and care for a child, because so many major changes occur and growth is so noticeable.

During toddlerhood, children move from almost complete dependence on adults and others to the beginnings of self-reliance. They can move fairly well, do things for themselves, and express themselves verbally and in other ways to get what they want.

Listening:
- Please read *Papa, Please Get the Moon for Me* by Eric Carle.

Dialogue:
- Discuss what was magical in the story for you. What parts do you think would be especially enjoyable to a toddler? Why?
- What is the toddler learning from the story in addition to the fact that Papa is trying to comply with Monica's wishes? (Discuss social and emotional learnings as well as cognitive ones.)

Action:
- Plan center materials and activities, appropriate for toddlers, based on the theme of this storybook. Remember, toddlers are very hands-on learners,

so the materials must be safe and durable. Plan a display of your theme centers with the class.
- Brainstorm ways that you see toddlers learning from each other and ways you see this learning reflecting theories about young children's learning. Report to your class.

In addition to becoming self-reliant, toddlers begin to learn and comply with the rules and values of society. They begin to be socialized. As children show that they can understand, social rules and values are actively imposed on them by parents and other. Learning theorists suggest that young children comply because they want to maintain closeness with parents and have their needs met.

As they grow more sociable, toddlers become more competent in their interactions with adults and with other children. They can observe and interpret the actions of others, imitate them, and maintain a sequence of interaction with others.

Listening:
- Think back to your earliest memories and write about a family member or loved one's facial expression that you *knew* what the expression meant—even as a very young child. Write about what you remember about the person, the context, and the situation. How did you know what that person meant?
- Now have some fun remembering some of the sounds of your childhood. What were the sounds? What made the sounds? Do you remember Grandfather's cane thumping as he walked through the house or apartment? Do you remember the ice cream truck? The raucous neighbors?
- Please read *Mr. Brown Can Moo, Can You: Dr. Seuss's Book of Wonderful Noises*.

Dialogue:
- What about this book relates to your own memories that you just wrote about? Please discuss this with your small group.
- In what ways does the author give the toddler an arena to observe and interpret the actions of others? Please discuss.

Action:
- Read the story to a small group of toddlers. Read the story again and again. Become an action researcher and jot down notes of children's behaviors and speech that show you they are taking something from that particular story. Share your notes with the class.
- Interview a family member, friend, or neighbor whom you know grew up in a different language environment in which English was not spoken. What

were some of the rhymes, stories, and songs? Try to document some examples and all class members bring back contributions to an "Emerging Language" Expo which is truly multilingual and multicultural.

During this stage, most toddlers begin talking; therefore, language development will demand much of our attention as we study this age group. In addition to learning words, toddlers begin to learn the rules, or conventions, for combining sounds into words and words into sentences. This is a fairly sophisticated process by itself, but it must be developed in the complexity of social situations that can change the rules, so it is an amazing accomplishment.

The first task in language development is learning sound patterns. In infancy, we hear babies cry and coo and babble, and toward the end of the first year, we hear patterned speech. It sounds like babbling, but it has a pattern to it that resembles the intonation and form of those around him. Once the toddler recognizes and can produce a small number of phonemes (groups of sounds, the smallest speech units), he begins to say his first words and to recognize words.

Listening:
• Please read *Brown Bear, Brown Bear, What Do You See?* by Eric Carle, illustrated by Bill Martin.

Dialogue:
• What are the aspects of this children's classic story that would appeal to a child developing language?

Action:
• Design and make some form of puppets based on this story. Try out your puppets with a toddler, or group of toddlers, who are fond of this story. Share your experiences.

Toddlers quickly develop expressive language, the ability to produce language forms. That development follows a sequence. The child begins with the language learning task—learning words and their meanings. The first words are, of course, the names of familiar people and items.

Early vocabulary also includes social commands, such as "Me"; movements, such as "Go, bye bye"; and expressions of "No." During this learning period, parents and others who interact with the toddler influence the range of vocabulary and how it is used. Adult language patterns will often determine the toddler's language patterns. For example, if a parent asks a great number of "What?" questions of the toddler, the toddler will develop extensive vocabulary to label things.

The average toddler develops vocabulary slowly until about age 18 months, then the acquisition of new words increases dramatically. Between one and two years of age, the range of new words learned is between 100 and 1,000 words. That wide range is another reminder of individual differences. During this phase of toddlerhood, we hear young children attempting to make plurals of their words, or changing the tenses. They make a lot of mistakes in the process, often causing adults to chuckle at the attempts.

For most of toddlerhood, children are in a one-word stage, meaning that their speech is limited to using one word at time. With their use of single words, however, toddlers may be communicating more than a simple label. For example, when a toddler points to her mother and says "Momma," she may simply be acknowledging her mother. But when she holds up her mother's book, and says "Momma," she may be saying "Momma's book," or when she tugs at her mother's hand and says "Momma," she may be saying "Momma, let's read." This is an example of a holophrase, and toddlers soon have a number of holophrases that communicate their needs and wants as well as enable them to hold a conversation with others. What you will learn about toddlers' speech is that you must not only listen well but you must also notice the situation, observe the toddlers' gestures, and be ready to guess. They want to talk to you, and their language development will be enhanced if you are able to respond appropriately to their early attempts at conversation. At around eighteen to twenty-four months of age, toddlers begin to put two words together into two-word sentences. They are usually very simple ideas and are generally expressed with a noun and a verb, and occasionally an adjective. Such sentences capture the gist of what the toddler wants to say, and adults again must maintain an awareness of the entire situation in order to interpret them appropriately.

As an early childhood professional, you will need to follow her example and be a very good listener. The stages of language development go beyond two-word sentences, because some toddlers continue to develop their language and use telegraphic sentences, joined sentences, and even occasionally overgeneralizations.

Along with the development of language that has such dramatic growth during toddlerhood, there is also the beginning of a capacity for representation. The children begin to use symbols to represent things. Language use is one example of this capacity, but another is seen in pretend play. For example, toddlers will pretend to ride a large rectangular block or to drink out of a cylinder block. Young toddlers will play with actual objects such as dolls, cars and trucks, and animals. Older toddlers (near two years) represent other things in their play-blankets and kitchen objects.

Listening:
- Think back to your own toddlerhood or think about a toddler you know. What are some interesting "representations" the child makes? Write about the imagination and design of play of this brilliant child. What does the child pretend is something else? What examples of language do you hear the child using?
- Please read *The Foot Book: Dr. Seuss's Wacky Book of Opposites*.

Dialogue:
- What aspects of the story appeal to you as an adult reading the book? What do you think will appeal to the child you just wrote about?

Action:
- Read the story to a group of toddlers and write a journal entry about what the toddlers responded to.
- Design and create some concrete learning activity materials for toddlers using the book as a thematic guide. Try out your materials with some toddlers and note and report on their responses.
- Go to the library and review language acquisition theories. Which aspects of the theories have you observed in the toddlers you know? Report on your findings.

It takes a great amount of experience or practice, so it is important to provide appropriate materials and activities for children at this age. At this time, the coordination of eyes and hands improves greatly, and the toddler begins to master tasks such as assembling simple puzzles, matching faces, and so on.

Toddlers do not have well-developed perceptual motor skills—that is, the combination of what they see and the body movements to match what they perceive. They often bump into furniture or each other, or they try to stuff large toys into bags that are smaller than the toy. When they move to music, most toddlers do not really move to the rhythm or beat; they just move their bodies. At this age, children simply are not ready to process the information that they are taking in with their ears or eyes or touch. There is, however, one aspect of their experience that toddlers begin to organize and acknowledge: awareness of body and gender.

Toddler body awareness usually extends to curiosity about the body parts of others, such as their parents, siblings, and others in their lives. This is also a time when a toddler is able to tell you whether she is a boy or a girl; however, the toddler also thinks that she can change her gender identity. According to a female toddler, for example, putting on a man's hat changes her into a male.

One of us still remembers a three-year-old's drawing of himself as a girl, accompanied by his description of "I'm going to be a girl when I grow up."

Listening:
- Think back to your own childhood and remember some of the pretend identities you gave yourself. Were you Amelia Earhart, Peter Pan, Harriet Tubman, Huck Finn? Write about this.
- Please read *I Look Like a Girl* by Sheila Hamanaka.

Dialogue:
- What identities in the book relate to your own memories? Discuss how you see this story with the art presentations as a positive experience for little girls and boys.
- Collect the materials you will need, obtain permission for the project, and read the story to a group of toddlers. Then, assist the toddlers make their own "I Look Like . . ." books. Report to the class about the experience.

All the developmental changes that occur during toddlerhood have implications for the adults who support these young children. Toddler curiosity and the beginnings of independence require specific environments and behaviors on the part of adults. First, there are issues of safety. In addition, these children are forming relationships, and their relationships with caregivers and educators is a critical one. The adults in the lives of toddlers need to be constant and committed to these youngsters. Toddlers are not yet good communicators, so adults need to know them well and be able to determine and respond to their needs and cues.

Bredekamp and Copple (1997) remind us, "A healthy toddler's inner world is filled with conflicting feelings—independence and dependence, pride and shame, confidence and doubt, self-awareness and confusion, fear and omnipotence, hostility and intense love, anger and tenderness, initiative and passivity" (p. 68). Those contrasts are a real challenge to the adults who intend to support the toddler. When toddlers feel that support, and know that they can count on those adults, they are able to face their own frustrations, struggles, and disappointments. Those adults need to make wise decisions about routines, schedules, and rules, so that they are a source of support to the toddler rather than a source of defeat.

References

Bredekamp, S. and Copple, S. (Eds.) (1997). *Developmentally Appropriate Practice in Early Childhood Programs*. Washington, DC: National Association for the Education of Young Children.

Carle, E. (1974). *Papa, please get the moon for me*. (Little Simon Board Book). New York: Simon and Schuster.

Case, R. and Okamoto, Y. (1996). The role of central conceptual structures in the development of children's thought. *Monographs of the Society for Research in Child Development* 61 (1–2, serial no. 246).

Caudill, W. and Frost, L. (1974). A comparison of maternal care and infant behavior in Japanese-American American, and Japanese families. In William P. Lebra (Ed.) *Youth, Socialization, and Mental Health, Vol. 3 of Mental Health Research in Asia and the Pacific*, Honolulu: University Press of Hawaii, p. 3.

Demi. (1995). *Demi's dragons and fantastic creatures*. New York: Henry Holt and Company.

Derman-Sparks, L. (1992). Reaching potentials through anti-bias, multicultural curiculum. In S. Bredekamp & T. Rosegrant (Eds.), *Reaching potentials: Appropriate curriculum and assessment for young children* (Vol. 1, pp. 114–128). Washington, DC: National Association for the Education of Young Children.

Driscoll, A. and Nagel, N. (2000). *Early childhood education, birth–8: The world of children, families, and educators*. New York: Allyn and Bacon.

Edwards, P. & Pleasants, H. & Franklin, S. (1999). *A path to follow: Learning to listen to parents*. Portsmouth, NH: Heinemann.

Frasier, D. (1991). *On the day you were born*. New York: Hartcourt Brace.

Gerber, M. (1988). *Respectfully yours: Magda Gerber's approach to professional infant/toddler care*. In Lally, J.R. (Executive Producer/Content Developer/Writer), Mangione P.L. (Content Developer/Writer), Signer, S. (Content Developer/Writer), & Butterfield, G.O. (Producer). (1988). *e* [Videotape]. United States: The Program for Infant/Toddler Caregivers.

Gonzalez-Mena, J. (1996). *Multicultural Issues in Child Care*. Mayfield Publishing.

Greenman, J. (October, 1989). Living in the real world: Diversity and conflict. *Exchange*, p. 1.

Hamanaka, S. *I look like a girl*. New York: Morrow Junior.

Joosse, Barbara M. (1991). *Mama do you love me?* New York: Scholastic Inc.

Katz, L. (1993). Dispositions as educational goals. Urbana, IL: ERIC Clearinghouse on Elementary and Early Childhood Education. (Catalog#211)

Kraus, R. (1994). *Leo the late bloomer*. New York: HarperCollins Juvenile Books.

Lubecks, S. (1994). The politics of developmentally appropriate practice. In B.L. Mallory and R. S. New (Eds.), *Diversity and developmentally appropriate practices*, pp. 17–43. New York: Teachers College Press.

Martin, B. & Carle, E. (1996). *Brown bear, brown bear, what do you see?* New York: Henry Holt.

New, R. (1994). Culture, child development, and developmentally appropriate practices: Teachers as collaborative researchers. In B. Mallory & R. New, *Diversity and developmentally appropriate practices*, pp. 65–83. New York: Teachers College Press.

Okamoto, Y., Case, R., Bleiker, C., and Henderson, B. (1996). Cross cultural investigations. In R. Case and Y. Okamoto, Eds., *The Role of Central Conceptual Structures in the Development of Children's Thought*. Monographs of the Society for Research in Child Development 61 (1–2, serial no. 246), pp. 131–155.

Seuss, Dr. (1996). *My many colored days* (The Board Book). New York: Knopf.

Seuss, Dr. (1996). *The foot book: Dr. Seuss's wacky book of opposites* (Bright & Early Board Book.) New York: Random House.

Seuss, Dr. (1970). *Mr. Brown can moo, can you?* (Bright & Early Board Book.) New York: Random House.

Swadener, B. B. (2000). *Does the village still raise the child? A collaborative study of changing child-rearing and early education in Kenya*. Albany, NY: SUNY Press.

· 5 ·

PROBLEM-POSING AND THE
PRESCHOOL YEARS

*I don't remember when I learned to read, but I knew it was before I started school
and it was from stories told by my family. I learned to read quite early. I loved
being read to when I was young. I still like to be read to. I had all sorts of books.
My parents read to me and so did my grandma. My grandma would read a whole
stack of books to me before bed. We would change the characters' names throughout
the books. When I started reading, I read my grandma to sleep. I would also
change all of the names on my own.*

Yes, preschool aged children know a lot and learn a lot more. When they
are supported and loved by families and teachers, they thrive—individually and along with their friends. It is during these years between
ages three and five that children expand their knowledge about their world.
They continue to notice when things are the same or different. They observe
and pretend to be adults, animals, and even inanimate objects. They continue
to visually identify shapes of objects and letters and identify and order specific
letters. Children begin to realize that words consist of individual letters.

Furthermore, children begin to make decisions for themselves, learn to
play with others and negotiate give-and-take relationships. And their physical
capabilities are expanding by leaps and bounds. Much of this learning happens
during play and during daily living activities among family and community.
When their learning is allowed to thrive in natural circumstances, they know
what they want to learn. It is immediately important that we as educators of
young children learn to observe and use what it is the children want to know.

Many early childhood educators are tuning in to variations of what is sometimes called "Emergent Curriculum" (Hendricks, 1998). In this method of
planning learning for young children the first step is to begin with an aspect of

the world that has caught the children's interest. Then the teachers usually brainstorm ideas about ways and things to teach the children that are related to the topic. Next, the teachers narrow down the possibility by facing the reality of what is possible and what is not. Then, teachers plan activities throughout the week. Finally, they fit activities into the daily schedule and evaluate what happened and decide how to improve the activity (Hendricks, 1998). Problem-posing using multicultural children's literature is a natural companion to emergent curriculum or in many ways it could be considered better because many aspects of culture, language, and art become the basis for noticing and supporting children's interests. Maybe even more importantly, children are encouraged to not only follow their own interests, but become critical creators of their worlds.

Children Become Critical Creators of Their Worlds

The early childhood classroom is a nexus for collaborative, integrative curriculum building. When there is an emphasis on child-centered, culturally inclusive approaches, the verbal and nonverbal communication, reading, writing, numeracy, science, social studies, the arts, and an expanded vision of technology can be encouraged. Using multicultural children's literature in a problem-posing format is the ideal framework to do this.

The beliefs, ideas, and history which underlie an integrated curriculum can be explored consistently as we plan activities using multicultural stories and the listening, dialogue, action format of problem-posing. The interrelationships among early childhood curriculum and large and small motor development, perceptual development, sensory-motor development, and aspects of daily living for young children become clear as we watch and interact with children in these activities. This is also true for the critical roles and interrelationships of the physical, temporal, psychological, and social environments in supporting development. As we journey through a few sample activities here in this chapter, the reader will see a developing competency in the design, implementation, and assessment of appropriate, anti-bias, integrated early childhood curriculum in the following areas: literacy, numeracy, technology, science, social studies, drama, visual arts, music and movement, and daily living.

How does the curriculum mediate the child's experiences? Why encourage a child-centered, integrated curriculum? These are important questions to keep in mind throughout this chapter and throughout the book. When planning for preschool aged children, the importance of each of the curriculum areas and how they interrelate must be addressed. Curriculum and instructional methodologies which are culturally and linguistically sensitive and appropriate for meeting the language, learning, and affective needs of a diverse population must be a part of our planning. Teachers are collaborators with children and parents and others to generate interest, uncover what the children already know and think about curriculum areas, and foster the emergence of new inquiry. For example, the various content areas will be studied through a process of observation, reflection, documentation, and activity development.

Teachers and student teachers often talk of early childhood experiences that have to do with interactions with family members and activities other than book-reading that influence their early learning. One man noted:

> My parents lived in Mexico, and then they crossed to the United States. I was born right on this side of the border. I have eight brothers and eight sisters. In the summer I would work every day from 5:00 AM till sundown. We didn't work during the school year except for weekends. . . . Everything was very positive. Your father is there; your mother is there; and your brothers and sisters are there too. You are all working together and your father is saying good things all day, every day for a long time. I didn't know at the time, but it was a close family unit. They talk about supporting a family now with low incomes. With the migrant families we were doing that long ago. (Quintanilla, 1997, p. 165)

Listening:
- Please write about what you remember about all your family members' hair. Do you remember your brothers hating to go for haircuts? Do you remember older sisters vying for time at the mirrors to "fix" their hair? How do these memories of hair help to define the person in your memory. Write about this.
- Draw a "family portrait" that puts special emphasis on family members' hair. Write a few lines describing the hair under the sketches.
- Listen to or read *Hairs/Pelitos* by Sandra Cisneros.

Dialogue:
- Please share your writings and/or drawings with a partner and discuss your stories along with the story by Cisneros.

Action:
- Find a photograph of some of the family members you wrote or drew about. Check your memories and expand on a memoir type short story to send to one of the family members as a gift.
- Plan "center" activities for a group of preschool age children around the family theme. What props would you supply in the pretend-play space?

The blocks area? The art area? The library? The science/nature area? The math area?

- Read the storybook *Tell Me Again about the Night I Was Born* by Jamie Lee Curtis (1996). The story is about the narrator's adoptive parents rushing to the hospital by airplane, to pick up their much awaited and already loved baby. Plan a short research project in which you gather information about the procedure of adoption in this country and others. Gather information about recommendations about discussing adoption and discussing birth parents with young children. There have been mixed reviews about this storybook because it mentions the birth mother. After you have compiled your information, report to your class.

Symbols of Meaning in Preschool Years

As adults living in various contexts and cultures around the work we attach meaning to symbols, different meanings to the same words, and even our own interpretations of artifacts such as flags and colors.

> Telling someone what a symbol meant was like telling them how a song should make them feel, it was different for all people. A white Ku Klux Klan headpiece conjured images of hatred and racism in the U.S., and yet the same costume carried a meaning of religious faith in Spain. (Brown, 2003, p. 35)

Of course, this meaning-making is important for children to figure out on their own terms. By using problem-posing with multicultural children's literature, we provide a safe and respectful arena for children to work out their own meanings for words and symbols.

Listening:
- Write about your name and if you know its meaning. Also write about who named you and who you may have been named for.
- Now remember a time when you were about five years old and you loved to pretend that you were someone or something else. What did you pretend? What do you remember about why you liked to do this?
- Read *My Name Is Yoon* by Helen Recorvits.

Dialogue:
- What stands out for you in terms of the strengths of Yoon? How does the story relate to what you wrote about your memories?

Action:
- Observe preschoolers at play when they are pretending. What do you notice about their play? Are they having fun? Are they working out any real-life issues? Are they reaching out to others? Are they using language and literacy and other forms of knowledge? In what ways? Report to your class.
- Research the work of Elliott Eisner, Tom Barone, Maxine Greene or other researchers who study the connections among creativity, the arts, and learning. Report to your class.
- Observe a group of children playing who do not speak the same language. What do you notice about their negotiations? Report to your class.
- Plan an action research project for a long-term investigation into community, family and school literacy environments, exploring theories about language acquisition in one or more languages and the relationship between oral and written language, studying children's social use of language, and studying the connections between story, multicultural children's literature, writing and reading. Maybe you will choose one student, like Yoon, to focus on for your learning. Or maybe you will study a small group of children who are friends to study these issues. It is important to get suggestions from your teacher about scholars who can inform you about the theoretical basis of these topics and about the new emphasis about reconceptualizing early childhood and early learning.
- Read the storybook *Charlie Parker Played Be Bop* by Chris Raschka. Plan a problem-posing lesson for preschoolers that combines this story, jazz, art, and biography and autobiography. Try out your plan and report to your class.

Realizing the importance of naming and identity for all humans, especially young children, many teacher education students seek out storybooks about the topic which may be used with different age groups of children. A teacher education student planned the following lesson for four- and five-year olds.

Listening:
- I would begin the lesson by playing a Native-American song for the class and then read them the storybook, . . . *If You Lived with the Cherokee* by Peter and Connie Roop, illustrated by Kevin Smith. I would then discuss the book and ask, "If you were a Cherokee, what would you name yourself and why?" Then I would ask the children to write or draw their Cherokee names in their writing notebooks using symbols or drawings.

Dialogue:
- If they had any questions about the book, we would discuss it and then we would discuss their names and why they chose them. I would ask them if

they knew what their "real" names meant or if they knew anyone who was a Cherokee. For example, my maiden name is Krizan and in Slovak that means "cross." I would prompt them with questions about what Cherokee customs and games were similar to modern day games and we'd discuss them. For example, the modern game of lacrosse came from a Cherokee version of stickball. We'd also talk about the treatment of Indians by the United States government and I'd ask children what they thought about it. I'd ask them if they ever knew anyone who was treated unfairly.

Action:
• Depending on the children's answers and what direction the conversation went, I would ask them to choose one aspect of Cherokee living that they related to most or that reminded them of their own heritage and bring in a representational object to class the next day. It could be anything from a stickball bat, jewelry, clothing, a food item, a picture of a house, and tools like a fishing pole. We would gather together like the Cherokee, I would review the book (maybe read it again or have them partner-read), and then we would listen to each other's stories about our objects. (The Cherokee didn't go to school in a building; they learned by listening to the older people in the village tell stories.) If the children brought in games similar to the Cherokee basket game, we could play it. I would finish by playing more Native-American music and maybe we would even dance by shaking rattles (if available) to the music like the Cherokee did during celebrations.

Language, not only the specific language our family speaks, such as Spanish, Cantonese, or English, but the dialect and forms of language, helps to define our identities and mark our membership in groups of communicators who have shared knowledge about shared meaning.

Listening:
• Think about the language you use in the company of very close friends or family. How is this different from the language you use at work? At school? Do the words you use define anything about your identity? Do the words reflect your beliefs about things? Does that language include any "secret codes or meanings? Write about this in your journal.
• Write about language used with young children in your family.
• Write about an experience in which you noticed a person's language was celebrating his/her identity.
• Listen to or read, *Be Boy Buzz* by bell hooks.

Dialogue:
- Discuss the storybook in terms of a child's identity. Discuss also the language used in the book. In what ways can you discuss poetic language with young children?

Action:
- Review any of the multitude of works by bell hooks. In what ways can you draw a connection between her philosophies and activism and the ideas expressed in this storybook?
- Collect classroom books by famous poets accessible on a "Poetry Spot" or table.
- Provide pictures from book to children so they may write a poem to be pasted on to the picture. At end of this activity students sit at the reading rug and share their poems
- Research and revisit early childhood models from the U.S.A. and Western Europe from Froebel, Pestallozi, Montessori to Head Start and Even Start Programs. What is the history? What have we learned from these models? Relate what you learn to what you have read and discussed so far in this book. Report to your class.
- Review the following Web sites and report to your class:

Froebel, http://asuwlink.uwyo.edu/~drow/new_page_3.htm

Pestallozi,http://translate.google.com/translate?hl=en&sl=pt&u=http://www.andi.org.br/midia_edu/perfis/pestalozzi.htm&prev=/search%3Fq%3Dpestallozzi%26hl%3Den%26lr%3D%26ie%3DUTF-8%26sa%3DG

Montessori, http://www.montessori-ami.org/ and http://www.amshq.org/

Weikhart, http://www2.acf.dhhs.gov/programs/hsb/research/

- Choose one or more of the following research reports about early learning to read and report back to your class about:

Barnett, W. S. (1996). *Lives in the balance: Age-27 benefit-cost analysis of the High/Scope Perry Preschool Program* (Monographs of the High/Scope Educational Research Foundation, 11). Ypsilanti, MI: High/Scope Press.

Ellsworth, J. & Ames, L. J. (Eds.). (1998). *Critical perspectives of Project Head Start: Revisioning the hope and challenge.* Albany, NY: SUNY Press.

Schweinhart, L. J., Barnes, H. V., & Weikart, D. P. (1993). *Significant benefits: The High/Scope Perry Preschool study through age 27* (Monographs of the High/Scope Educational Research Foundation, 10). Ypsilanti: High/Scope Press.

Sarmento, T., Bandeira, A., Nunes, G., & Baptista, I. (2002*). Childhood House—centre of action-research with children*, Lisbon, Portugal. Presentation at Fourth Warwick International Early Years Conference, Warwick, England.

Preschoolers and Literacy

In terms of just literacy skills alone, preschool aged children have expanded their vocabulary from 4000 words to 6000 words and show more attention to abstract use of words. They use verbal commands to claim things and use language to tease. They quickly learn new vocabulary when it is related to their own experiences and can retell a four or five step story in sequence. Preschoolers understand that print carries a message, and can use identifying labels and signs in the environment (Seefeldt & Galpre, 2000). But of course, these understandings of the literacy process begin early in life. They usually happen a bit differently for each of us, but almost always with a connection to a significant person, a significant place and time. Let's stop for a moment so you may think about your own memories. Family, defined as all those loved ones we lived with and live with now, are always of utmost importance.

Autobiographical Narrative about Early Literacy

In all of these "Listening" sections of our activities, the self-reflection, autobiographical aspect of problem posing encourages us as students to use imagination and metaphor as the work to connect experiences in their own lives as a part of a family and a community to the information being addressed in the class. Teacher education students in an early childhood/elementary literacy class reflected on their earliest memories of reading and how that personal experience was tied to experiences with family members and loved ones. Some reflections were:

> I remember being really young and just loving to look at books and hold them. Before I could read, I can recall making up the story and pretending that I was saying the actual words on the page. This curiosity was clearly brought about by having my mom or grandmother read to me. That was my first encounter with books, and served to spark my interest.

And another student acknowledges important memories.

> I fondly recall my aunt S. who was a teacher and bought me my very first book. It was a picture dictionary of a magical world of words. It was geared to help a child

through the mediums of art and colorful illustrations. I also remember looking forward to bedtime as that meant my mother would read to me. This in fact is my earliest recollection of noticing words and letters. I began to recognize letters and form words which in turn created a sense of excitement and creativity. With encouragement at home I first learned to read and I now comprehend the significant importance of an early and pleasant introduction to books. In my opinion, reading is the essential key to a life long learning experience.

And, then an individual storybook leaving the mark of a lifetime is described:

I can still visibly picture my favorite page of the book I adored as a child, with the little blue train struggling so hard to make it to the top of the hill. "I think I can, I think I can, I think I can." I can even see the words written in black bold print on the top of the page. Memories of my first reading experience involve my favorite storybook of all time, *The Little Engine That Could*. I must have been about three or four years old. I loved the story so much that I had every person in my family read it to me, time and time again. I could not read it on my own, nor did I pretend to read it, but I would recite the story, almost word for word, along with whoever read it to me. Hearing the story read aloud would jog my memory and eventually, I came to recognize the famous four words, "I think I can." Learning what the words looked like came from seeing and hearing them so much and also by associating them with the picture. I believe learning those words also had to do with the way they were read to me in a whisper that gradually got louder and louder. The words sounded full of courage and excitement, and it was the sound of the words that drew my attention to them. Now that I think of it, it was a combination of things that encouraged me to learn my first words; the way the words sounded, the fact that my family took the time to read with me, the colorful pictures, the large, bold easy-to-read print and my fascination with the storyline. It happened naturally. I learned to read my first words because I wanted to. I was able to read those four words before I formally learned to read. Over exposure to hearing and seeing words combined with the love of family and the love for a story book can make all the difference in a child's literacy life.

In addition, as a part of the autobiographical narrative focus and our study of how children learn to read, students had been asked to reflect upon their memories about how early experiences with reading were influenced by a teacher. One response was:

I really don't remember exactly how I learned to read but I do remember my reading experiences in second grade. It was in second grade, where I really began to wonder if I was ever going to succeed. I wasn't only challenged by my new school but placed in a regular English class for the first time. I was so frightened during the first few weeks until Mrs. S. my reading lab teacher walked into my life. I had reading lab hour every day of the week. During our small group meetings, we used to review the different strategies available to sound a word out and to find its meaning. She tried to connect new words with words we already knew. She also taught us to look for clues or hints in the context of the sentence that might help us understand the meaning of the word. I remember once she gave me a puzzle of a poem, which described a beautiful princess sailing around the world and my first thesaurus, *In Other Words.*

Varied Ways of Knowing

As an aspect of the structure of this research study, feminist theory and other theories that are seen in our literature, our lives and our worlds were approached with the students. We discussed and explored the many perspectives about learning and life that are portrayed through multicultural children's literature. For example, we can learn about native perspectives on healing by a curandera (healer) in several of Gloria Anzaldúa's children stories, we can learn about legends of creation from native peoples of Central America through Subcommandante Marcos's *Book of Colors*, we can learn about Inuit people's ideas about life cycles in *Northern Lights: The Soccer Trails* by Michael Arvaarluk Kusugak. These perspectives are important to include in the early childhood curriculum and through the multicultural children's literature, teachers and children can explore the ideas in age-appropriate ways.

Listening:
- Write about your memories of a creation story or a story about the creation of a certain place that was dear to you, or a story about animals, people, or places that seemed fantastic to you as a young child.
- Read about the history of the Zapatistas and their political struggle in Chiapas, Mexico. The people there are fighting to conserve their culture and a vision of the world which they see as flowering with holiness. Their vision of holiness is different from that of many people in the United States.
- Read *The Story of Colors/La Historia de los Colores* by Subcomandante Marcos.

Dialogue:
- In small groups discuss your initial reactions to the story.
- Now, see if you can make some broad connections between this story and your stories you wrote about above.

Action:
- Plan some activities for young children that focus on identity, collaboration, community building, and negotiation of conflicts. Make sure each

child's ideas about identity and reality are supported and respected. Probably a focus on art opportunities and pretend play are a good place to begin. Also, integrate some of the sensory-motor approaches developed by Maria Montessori and other approaches which are based on hands-on learning experiences in relation to earth science, and cycles of growth and change, and the relationships of natural phenomena to all areas of study. Observe children as they interact with these activities and each other. Make an action plan for more integrated curriculum and share with your class.

Family traditions support children and encourage their emotional and social development while their literacy and cognition grow and flourish.

Listening:
- Write about a situation in which you were very sad about the loss of a loved one. Who helped you work through it? How did that person help you? How did you help yourself? How did your community help you?
- Write about a folktale, legend, or family story that has for one purpose the teaching of comfort at a time of loss.
- Read the story *Northern Lights: The Soccer Trials* by Michael Arvaarluk Kusugak.

Dialogue:
- How did the story portray the happiness and sadness of the character's life in an integrated way? How did the ancient beliefs of her people become personalized for her? Discuss the intersection of science, art, and belief in this story.
- Discuss any connections you can make between your own stories and the story of Kataujag.

Action:
- Investigate selected historical curriculum approaches that focus on the arts including, the Waldorf/Steiner Approach, the Reggio Emilia Approach and the beliefs and documentation regarding the importance of creative play and art activities. What are some ideas you have that could be used along with story that were stimulated by reading about the various project-based approaches you studied? Try out your ideas and report to your class about what happened.

If you were raising questions in the previous activities, about whether or not we should be discussing issues of death and the afterlife with children, you are not alone. These questions often come up in teacher education classes about the addressing of difficult issues with the children. Should discussions about divorce, death, fear, and loneliness be a part of our work with young children? Actually, there is much research that advises that we (once trust is developed within the community of learners and always in dialogue with our students' families) answer children's questions and acknowledge their sometimes oblique references to these issues through their art work or pretend play.

Again Grace, of *Amazing Grace* fame, can be useful in addressing aspects of step-families and being far away from a loved one.

Listening:
- Write about a family member who lives far away from you (now or in your childhood). How do you communicate with that person? What pictures of that person in that far away place come to your mind?
- Write about the details of a blended family you know. How do the various family member negotiate ways to be together and to be apart?
- Read *Boundless Grace: Sequel to Amazing Grace* by Mary Hoffman.

Dialogue:
- Discuss Grace's family's arrangements. Discuss the different characters' contributions to the relationships.

Action:
- Interview at least three people about being a part of a single parent family or a blended family. Always begin with a question about the positive aspects of the situation and then follow with questions about barriers and difficulties. Be sure to ask permission to share information in your class groups and be sure to guarantee anonymity to the interview informant.
- Research in an academic source some information and guidelines regarding single parent families, blended families, and step families. Write a short report that documents a synthesis of facts, current opinions in the culture which was studied, and your own opinions of what you learned.

Legend and Folktales in Children's Lives

Children's literature author, Lunge-Larsen (1999), reminds us of the importance of literature in children's lives. She has researched folk tales and legends from around the world and has been telling stories to young children for over 20 years. She often says that in a world in which children are exposed to confusing and shifting realities and values, folk tales and legends serve as a ". . . rudder. They touch eternal truths about how to live that will never become irrelevant" (p. 10).

It is useful for teachers to explore folktales and the cultural perspectives from which they come.

Listening:
Read the following information about trolls in literature and legend.

> Trolls are giants shaped by the ancient Norse mythology and by the towering Scandinavian landscape. Clearly, one aspect of children's fascination with trolls is that they make the very landscape come alive. . . . But perhaps the greatest reason children love troll stories is because children need stories like them. Nothing can truly show children, even adults, more about how to live, about who they are, and about their place in the world, and the struggles of life than a good folktale, and these troll stories I count among the best . . . As a society we have come to think of folktales as amusing entertainment, quaint relics of the past. We certainly do not view them as vehicles for understanding. Yet folktales explore issues as complex as the nature of good and evil, and the triumph of kindness and patience over bullying and anger. Folktales reveal universal truths. . . . (Lunge-Larsen, 2002, pp. 3–4)

- What is a legend or folk tale or family yarn that you remember from your childhood? Describe all the details of the story that you remember. Describe the person who usually told you the story. Where were you during the telling? Did the story incite any particular feelings and actions after it was told? What were they?
- Read *Prietita and the Ghost Woman/ Prietita y la Llorona* by Maya Christina Gonzalez and Gloria E. Anzaldúa.
- Read *Maya's Children: The Story of La Llorona* by Rudolfo Anaya.

Dialogue:
- Discuss the legends. What aspects of the cultural and political history of the region where this legend originated do you know?
- Discuss ways this legend relates to your childhood memories of legends.

Action:
- Research legends of a country that you know very little about. Some suggestions may be Turkey, Malaysia, Vietnam, Serbia, Nicaragua, Saudi Arabia. Choose a legend that you like and prepare a creative way to share it with the class. As a part of your presentation, document some political, social, and cultural facts that you believe are evident in the legend.
- Visit an art museum and choose a painting that you are moved by that may depict some sort of legend. Research the painting in terms of legend, myth, and social history. Report to your class.

Teacher Education Students Implementing Problem-posing with Children

As previously mentioned, a few weeks after having participating in problem-posing with multicultural children's literature, and having read and discussed examples of my using this method with a Head Start class and a first grade class (Chapter 1), the students began to work on their own problem-posing with young children in their classrooms.

Students Planning Problem-Posing with Multicultural Children's Literature

ROUGH DRAFT (Problem-posing with Pre-K)

For this lesson, I have selected a collection of 22 bilingual poems written by the Mexican poet Francisco X. Alarcón, *From the Bellybutton of the Moon and Other Summer Poems.* In preparing the class for this lesson, the poem 'From the Belly-button of the Moon 1 & 2' should be posted up on opposite walls of the classroom. Pictures made by the children of activities they do with their family or special trips they have taken with their family should be posted next to these poems. The making of these pictures can be a separate activity done in advance. The children will be eager (especially in my class) to share pictures of their family/trips and are in fact even doing them now. There is only one girl in my class that is Mexican, S-E. She is also Cuban. I think that she will definitely be able to relate to the lesson and be excited about sharing her life with her classmates. It is also important to incorporate this lesson into the general curriculum of the class. The children are learning about where they come from. They have studied babies, their school, their neighborhoods, and now they are learning about their homes. My cooperating teachers are now conducting home visits where 4–5 students visit the home of their classmate. During this visit they learn about their classmate's home life, family, and culture. This collection of poems is particularly relevant because it is about Francisco's childhood and what he learned about Mexico from his family. The children are given 45 minutes during the morning to participate in Work Time. They are given several options to choose from for their daily activity. For this lesson, I would like to incorporate the poetry and/or Mexican culture in each of the activities. If at all possible it would be an added benefit to have someone from S-E's home come and speak to the children. This would have to be discussed and worked out by the cooperating teacher.

Listening:
- During morning meeting, before the children begin work time, I would take down or call their attention to the poems posted on the walls. I will ask them to:

1. First talk about the pictures they made of their family and trips,
2. Remind the class about what the poems were about. The poems would have been discussed in the preliminary activity.

• Next, I would take out a tape that I recorded of myself reading the poems section by section in Spanish and English and play it for them. I will also have created illustrations to complement the story. The children will listen to the story and look at the pictures as I hold them up for each section of the story. The poems are *Green Grass, Sunflower,* and *Rainbow* (by Francisco X. Alarcón.)

Dialogue:
• At the end of the poems, I will stop the tape and I will ask S-E, my four-year-old co-teacher, to share an object (or maybe a person) that is special to her that reminds her of Mexico. For the rest of the students, I will ask "What do you think of when you hear the 'home' or 'school' or . . ." and follow the lead of the children's responses and questions. This discussion will lead the class toward an opportunity to express their thoughts in various Work Time activities.

Action:
• There will be several options for work time. S-E and I will explain the various "Work Time" choices. These choices will be posted in print and with a picture so that S-E will have an easier time remembering what they are when she announces them.

1. Audio-visual: Students may take turns recording their own poems, beginning with the words, "Whenever I say. . ."
2. Reading: Students may read some of the other poems in the book or choose from other bilingual books that have been put on display in advance.
3. Dramatic play: The children may take turns acting out some of the poems.
4. Writing: The students can write their own poems about their families and culture.

What Happened?

This student reported that on the day of her work with this lesson, it was raining and stormy so she couldn't take the children outside before the lesson as she had hoped. So, she brought in a big sunflower plant in a pot (to go with the Sunflower poem) and a huge green "grass" (plastic, like for sports games) mat and asked the children to take off their shoes and pretend that they were outside in the grass (to go with the Green Grass poem). Then she conducted the lesson as planned in her description. She brought in to our class three of the poems created by the four-year-olds and dictated to her as a part of the "Action" section of her lesson. The poems show the children's involvement.

Spring

by KJ and C.

There's a sun in a flower.
A bird came in the flower and
took the sun away.
And the bird put it up to the sky.
The rain came down
and the bird got wet and he
rushed home and he
broke the sun's heart.
And the sun was never the same again.
The next day it wasn't raining
and the bird came back
The flowers bloomed
and the sun came back
He said, "Oh, what a gorgeous day."
When the sun came back he jumped
for joy and sang his song.

C's Song

Once there was a kitten
and every night he liked to curl up in
the bed and one day the kitten
    tripped off the bed.
He tried to jump back on but couldn't.

KJ's Poem

When you see me in the Spring time
I always see you.
You should say my name.
I will love you.
You should say what I say
It never is the truth
to say ma . . . ah.
Oh . . . oh . . . oh. . .
Halleluiah.

Yes, Halleluiah, and thank you preschoolers for showing us.

References

Alarcón, F. X. (1998*). From the belly button of the moon and other summer poems: Del ombligo de la luna.* San Francisco, CA: Children's Book Press.

Anaya, R. (1997*). Maya's children: The story of La Llorona.* New York: Hyperion Books.

Anzaldúa, G. (1995). *Prietita and the ghost woman.* San Francisco, CA: Children's Book Press.

Brown, D. (2003). *The DaVinci code.* New York: Doubleday.

Colectivo Callejero (1996) *The Story of Colors/La Historia de los colores: A folktale from the jungles of Chiapas.* Hong Kong: Creative Printing Limited.

Curtis, Jamie L. (1996). *Tell me again about the night I was born.* New York: Harpercollins Juvenile Books.

Hendrick, J. (1998). *Total learning: Developmental curriculum for the young child.* NJ: Merrill Education.

Hoffman, M. (1995). *Boundless Grace.* New York: Penguin Putnam.

Kusugak, Michael A. (1999). *Northern lights: The soccer trials.* Buffalo, NY: Annick Press.

Lunge-Larsen, L. (1999). *The troll with no heart in his body and other tales of trolls from Norway.* Boston: Houghton Mifflin Company.

Quintanilla, R. (1997). In Rummel, M. K. & Quintero, E. P. *Teachers' reading/Teachers' lives.* Albany, NY: SUNY Press.

Roop, Peter and Connie . . . *If You Lived with the Cherokee.*

Seefeldt, C. & Galpre, A. (2000). *Active Experiences for Active Children: Literacy Emerges* Columbus, OH: Prentice Hall.

·6·

KINDERGARTENERS
EXPLORING THE WORLD

*The first memory that I have of reading on my own is from kindergarten.
I recall working with the alphabet books in both English and Hebrew
and reading the small words like cat mostly through association with
the picture that was beside the printed words.*

Children in kindergarten are usually full of energy and excitement about school. This is the year when much of the foundations in reading, writing and math are being established. It is a challenge being a teacher who is trying to provide the children with a quality foundation and love for learning that will be carried with them and help them as they progress through school. While it is exciting to see them grow so much in a year, one of the challenges for teachers is to keep up the children's confidence in their abilities. A student told me recently, " . . . it is exciting when they first come in at the beginning of the school year and barely know how to read and write and by the end of the school year they are writing and reading."

Balanced Literacy, Kindergarten Curriculum, and the Big Picture

Curriculum guidelines and names for approaches change over time depending on new research, politics, and policy. In many districts in New York City currently, the buzz word for literacy and the method that literally becomes the entire curricular focus is "balanced literacy." What is it? It is a combination of many of the aspects of process methods which were introduced under the category of "whole language" and some of the other methods of more direct instruction such as phonics lessons. The name implies balance of all the methods. Some of the methods include shared reading, guided reading, running records, shared writing, guided writing, and using assessment and evaluation. The good thing about classrooms under the mandate to use balanced literacy is that the framework lends itself to integrated curriculum using children's literature. A student teacher described what she had learned in her classroom at her field site:

> I have learned a lot since I've been student teaching in Kindergarten. I have learned about the balanced literacy program that is used in my district, and have practiced each component, including shared reading, independent reading, guided reading, writer's workshop, interactive writing, and read-alouds. I have learned how independent children are, and that when they know their routine, they work so well. There are so many different ways for children to learn, and important that they are aware of what makes them a good reader and writer. . . . I learned about inventive spelling, which I had never seen before, and with that that when students have guidance, but are not discouraged, they are more willing and able to take risks with their writing, as well as their reading. I have been practicing assessment techniques, and have learned that there are so many different ways to assess students, and it is key to be aware of which ones work best for each child.

The teacher education students realize that in spite of all their learning about subject area information, child development, and their own background knowledge, things do not always go as planned and they must make intellectual decisions based on their observations of the children, their overall view of the "big picture" of the learning environment, and the individual needs of each child. This is the mix that makes teaching a rewarding, and sometimes daunting, challenge.

A student, who reflected on her experiences in the following statement, has begun to grasp the priorities in terms of the "big picture."

> In terms of the classroom and relationships, I've learned that the classroom works and runs much better when it is set up as a community, where it is safe to take risks. If sharing and working together is part of the class climate, it will show. Students will understand that to work in a group means sharing, and therefore learn the concept of teamwork. It is important to encourage positive relationships in the classroom, and that the students work actively together, both in whole and small group activities.

More Problem-posing by Student Teachers and Children

Relatedly, another student planned the following problem-posing activity for a group of five-year-olds.

Listening:

- Begin a discussion with a group of children (on the rug, perhaps) by asking them what they have done so far that day (or over the weekend, or yesterday, etc.) After the children answer, the teacher and the children will discuss what they think it means to be a kid. As the children talk about the story and relate it to their previous discussion, the teacher will write children's ideas on a flip chart in list format. The teacher will ask the children whether or not they think children of other countries do those same things.
- Read *To Be a Kid* by Maya Ajmera and John Ivanko.

Dialogue:

- Discuss the story and relate to children's ideas listed above. Discuss what surprised you about any of the story or pictures.

Action:

- Invite the children to use the collage materials to make a mural of all the things they think children do. The teacher can use the list that has been recorded to remind the children of their responses.

What Happened?

I did this lesson with the five-year-old age group at my school, with a few modifications and it went really well. I did the lesson during their work time, which is the time that centers are open, and they can go around the room to different centers. I first read the book to a group of about six children, though children were drifting in and out of my group during the whole activity.

Before I read the book I talked to the children, and asked them what fun things they did, that made them kids. They came up with a bunch of activities, several of which were in the book. I asked them if they thought that kids in other countries did those same things, and they said they didn't think so. After that conversation, we read the book. They were absolutely ecstatic to see that kids in other countries did indeed do those same activities that they name, and they wanted to know what country each picture was from, and if they were actually doing the same things. It was wonderful. After we talked about that, I had them add to a big mural about the activities kids all over the world do. I wrote "Kids all over the world . . ." in big letters in the middle, and then they drew pictures all around it. They dictated to me the captions for their pictures, such as "Kids all over the world paint different kinds of pictures," and "Kids all over the world look out windows and climb trees." As the original kids in the group slowly drifted away, and the other kids in the class came to join us, I looked through the book with the new kids, and invited them to draw a picture to go in our mural, which they did.

I thought that the lesson went really well, especially since the kids didn't know before how similar children all over the world can be. They really got the point of the book, and they were really excited about it. The mural they made is beautiful, and it is up on the wall in the classroom now.

It is no surprise that the best way for children to understand some of the "big picture" issues regarding multicultural appreciation and learning is through tangible, concrete learnings that involve people they know. The following student teacher used a connection between this multicultural story by Patricia Polaccio and a girl in the class who has relatives in Russia.

Listening:
- "Can anyone tell me where S. went last month? What do you know about Russia? S. can you give us a little background? Do you know about Pysanky eggs? Here are some pictures of these eggs and some history of where these eggs came from, how to make them, and what they were for. Pysanky eggs are symbols of new life in the Ukranian culture and are used as a decoration for holidays.
- Listen to the story *Pysanky Eggs* by Patricia Polaccio.

Dialogue:
- While reading, ask children to look at the pictures and talk about what certain words might mean.
- After reading, ask children: "Does anyone know someone like Miss Eula? Have you ever done something nice for a special friend? How did it feel? What did you notice in the stories (pictures) that were different or things that you've never seen before? Was it hard to understand the Russian words in the story? How do you think the children felt when they were blamed for something they didn't do? How did working together help the children?"

Action:
- Even though a real Pysanky egg is made with wax, we'll do it a little differently. Students will make and decorate plastic eggs (covered in contact paper—need a day to dry) for someone special in their lives. I'll also ask them to notice some of the patterns in the way the eggs are decorated.
- Students may also write a little about the time they worked together with someone else to achieve a goal or when someone did something nice for them or they did something nice for someone else.
- We might ask S.'s parents to come in and show some Russian items (either things in the book or something else). Let them talk about what it's like live in Russia and what they did when they were in kindergarten.

Please note in the following report of what happened, that in spite of a relatively well-thought out plan, there were some things the student learned about how she might do the activity differently next time.

What Happened?

Before I read the book, I tried to introduce Russian culture to the students by asking, "Can anyone tell me where S. went for her vacation a few months ago?" A lot of hands went up and they all knew that S. had taken a trip to Russia. I think I could have taken some time then, to talk about Russia and ask S. to talk about her trip but instead, I just started reading. Honestly, I don't think most of them know anything about Russia, therefore, I don't think the words or the pictures, or event the Pysanky eggs really made an impact on them. I think it would have helped tremendously for the students to have this background in order appreciate the wonderful way Patricia Polacco integrates Russian culture into the book. By exploring different aspects of the country, and giving the students a better understanding of the Russian culture, it also makes it easier for students to connect with the characters and enjoy the story even more. (Do you know anybody who is from Russia? What are they like?)

When we came across Russian words like "babushka," I asked if they could tell what it meant by how the story was told. They had no problem figuring out that "babushka" meant grandma. I had planned to talk abut Pysanky eggs before I started story, but I thought it might be more meaningful if they saw pictures first in the book. When the story went on to show how the kids made Pysanky eggs for Mr. Kodinski, I asked S. if she's seen these eggs before. She said she hasn't, but other students said they have. Other students started a conversation about how they made the eggs with wax and other times they decorated eggs (i.e. Easter). In the class, we actually did an art project by covering plastic eggs with contact paper and then decorating them. I reminded the children of what we did and I talked about how it's kind of similar. I probably did too much of the talking.

After the story, I tried to lead a discussion about helping other people and doing nice things for people who are nice to you, but I found it to be really hard. When I asked if they had ever wanted to do something nice for someone else, they all nodded. And the conversation ended there. It was hard for me to get the group to do more talking. This was only the first read, so I'm not too upset by the things I didn't do. I think it might be more helpful if we read the story again some other time and then go over the details.

On the next read, we can talk about the geometric designs on the eggs and perhaps I can bring in pictures of real Pysanky eggs to show the class. I don't know if I'd want the students to make the eggs with contact paper because they've already done a similar project. Instead, I think a good continuation after studying designs on the egg would be to ask the students to draw their own eggs and write a little about whom they would give the egg to and why. The students may come back and share afterwards. This should follow a conversation about how we can show people we care about them or what we do when someone's really nice to us.

Again, teacher education students realize the importance of building on children's personal experiences as a point of departure for new lessons. Another student, combining the learning aspects of sharing family stories with geography and social studies, planned the following lesson:

Begin the lesson by showing them a map of the world. Discuss different countries around the world.

Listening:
- Listen to the children report where they are from.
- Ask the children to draw or write about their country or culture.
- Listen to the book, *Whoever You Are* by Mem Fox.

Dialogue:
- Discuss the children's drawings or writing about their countries. The teacher asks questions about the different cultures such as different hobbies/crafts, holidays, family customs.

Action:
- Encourage children to explore nonfiction books, pictorial representations, magazines, maps and other informative documents in a world learning center so that children may continue learning about the country they began to talk and write about.
- Ask the children to plan a way to make a report about their learnings either by making a book, a puppet show, a skit, or a mural.
- If the children speak a different language at home, have those children teach the class a few simple phrases or vocabulary words such as hello, good bye, thank you, how are you, mom, dad, sister, brother.
- Have celebrations of countries and cultures that children have represented.

History, Art, and Activist People

An excellent way to lead into a study of famous people from a historical, artistic, and human rights standpoint, as well as a way to use all aspects of balanced literacy, is to begin with either the storybook *Frida* or the storybook *Diego*.

Listening:
- Think back to your early childhood years and remember an activity you were passionate about. Write about how you spent your time in doing this activity and include details about the context. How did you learn to "do" this activity? How did you become "good" at doing it? Were there other people involved in your learning? If yes, in what ways were they involved?
- Read *Diego* by Jeanette Winter.

Dialogue:
- With a partner, discuss the story about Diego Rivera and relate any aspects you can from his story to yours that you wrote about previously.
- Discuss how you would encourage the children to talk about what they like to do and how they express themselves. Diego expressed himself through art. How do you express yourself?

Action:
- In a kindergarten classroom, plan and implement a Diego Bulletin Board on which children constantly are contributing ideas (mirroring the chalkboard walls in the story). During Writing Workshop suggest children write about what children have drawn.
- In a kindergarten classroom, plan a map activity, "Where am I from? Where's my family from?"
- Investigate art history and history books to inform yourself about the historical context in which Diego Rivera lived and worked. Why was his hero Zapata? Why was he a colleague of Trotsky? Why are his murals in various national buildings in Mexico City considered a national treasure? Report to your class and make an action plan about how you could relay this historical information to kindergarteners.
- Read the children's storybook *Frida*. View the film *Frida*. Considering the context in which she lived, including her accident and including her marriage to Diego Rivera, how did she embody feminist ideals? How did she maintain her allegiance to what she believed to be most important? Report to your class and make an action plan about how you could relay this historical information to kindergarten students.
- Choose a figure in history that you admire. Frida Kahlo, Leonardo da Vinci, Amelia Earhart, Charlotte Brontë, J. R. R. Tolkien, Shakespeare, Harriet Tubman, Paulo Freire, or anyone you admire. Research that person's childhood experience and write a report about her/him and try to answer some of the questions you answered about yourself in the listening section of this section. (Your report could be in the form of a children's book like *Diego*.)

- Read, Ancona, G. (1998). *Barrio (Jose's Neighborhood)*. CA: Harcourt, Brace, & Company. Also available in Spanish: *Historias de mi barrio: el San José de ayer.* This is a book about the Mission District in San Francisco. It contains photographs and text which discuss the traditions, customs, art, food, etc. of what the locals call El Barrio. The book does this by following the goings-on of El Barrio through the life of one boy, Jose, and his elementary school. Read the following problem-posing lesson planned by a student teacher using this story.

Listening:
- The teacher and children learn about murals and what they are. The teacher then shows the children photos of murals from around the teacher's neighborhood. Children are given time to discuss the murals and ask questions.

Dialogue:
- What can you say about the neighborhood that these photos were taken in?
- What stories do these murals tell?
- If there are there murals in your neighborhood, please describe them for us.

Action:
- The teacher reads only the first half of *Barrio* with the class. This area of the book addresses murals and other forms of artistic expression (dance, song, etc.).

Listen:
- Then children might tell stories—through murals or other types of artistic expression (dance, song, etc.)—about themselves, their neighborhoods, etc.

Action:
- Children would decide to either partner up, get into a group, or work individually to create a mural, song, dance, etc. telling a story that they would like to share with the class.
- That evening the children would go home with a letter explaining the day's art activity and suggest that the family create a mural or other form of artistic expression which tells a story about their family. As the children returned with their family projects, extension activities would be implemented.
- Children would also be encouraged to bring in photos of murals or other forms of artistic expression from their own neighborhoods. Again, this activity would be accompanied by follow-up discussions and extension activities.

Now, we go back to balanced literacy and some of the methods the student at the opening of this chapter reported. Writing workshop, reading workshop, shared reading, read alouds and so forth are, of course, an important part of a first grader's learning. Yet, many experts (Avery, 1998; Calkins, 1994; Graves,

1994) tell us that these methods must be employed in the natural context of the child's life. Following, a story from Egypt, reminds us how this can be done.

Listening:
- Think back to your childhood and write about a "chore" or responsibility you had that took you out in to your community. Describe the chore. Describe the context of your community—what were the sounds, the smells, the visual details? Who were the people you encountered on your journeys? What skills did you learn through the experiences?
- Read *The Day of Ahmed's Secret* by Ted Lewin.

Dialogue:
- With a partner, discuss the story about Ahmed and relate any aspects you can from his story to yours that you wrote about previously.

Action:
- Read about children learning to write their name for the first time. Some places to begin looking for an appropriate article are journals from the National Associations for Young Children, The Association of Childhood Education International, the National Council for Teachers of English, and Teachers of English of Speakers of Other Languages, and the National Association of Bilingual Education. These and other professional organizations have informative Web sites.
- Plan a map quest or a scavenger hunt in your city. Plan to document the sounds of the city, the visual literacy of the city, the architecture of the city and the people of the city. With a group of children, plan to present what you learned to either a group of parents or other students.
- Read the following student response:

> I think what I reaped the most from our readings is that you can make any kind of lesson out of any kind of reading.
>
> We looked at *The Day of Ahmed's Secret*. I found so many lessons in this short story. For older children there can be a geography lesson, perhaps a trip to a museum. To help facilitate critical thinking we can connect the Cairo in the book to ancient Egypt. If there is an Egyptian child in the class he can be the host of a question and answer period where both the students and the teacher are equivalent participants. A writing workshop can be done on a variety of subjects such as sights and sounds of my city, the animals where I live, the desert. The possibilities are endless.
>
> I have also thought about younger children. Perhaps making a child-created bulletin board in a fours or fives classroom out of who can write their name, a significant achievement for these children and a way to get them motivated to learn how.

For young children I would have them use different media to reproduce what they saw or express their thoughts.

Another student teacher planned the following problem-posing activity that combines multicultural literature and science learning.

Listening:
- Listen to classmates tell about how families work together and help each other. How do you help out in your family? Do you take care of siblings? Do you help cook or clean?
- Read the story *Ma Jiang and the Orange Ants*, by Barbara Ann Porte (2000) which is a story set in ancient China about a young girl who helps her family first by taking care of the baby and then by taking over the job of her brothers and father when they are forced to become soldiers.

Dialogue:
- The children discuss the story and relate it to their lives. The teacher asks, "What was the role of the Orange Ants in this story? Why were they important?"

Action:
- Children write and draw about their role in the family.
- Re-read story, paying attention to role of ants. We also read follow-up text as suggested in back of book, such as *The Ancient Cultured Citrus Ant* or *Biological Pest Control*. This can introduce an ecosystems lesson in science. We can explore inter-dependence of animals and how people rely on animals as well as how they rely on each other.
- Students read in small groups from various animal books and try to discover how two different animals depend on each other. They can make drawings and charts to relay this information to the rest of the class.

Poetry and Kindergarten

If we want to encourage children to use language to create new images for themselves in cultural contexts, we need to know how to guide children's voices through reading and writing in expressive genres like fiction, poetry and creative nonfiction. We can teach children to be attuned to the voices of the writers they read and to listen with new ears to their own lives. "Poetry," Donald Graves (1994) says, "engages us in that penetrating moment when we see in a way that we didn't see before." Other types of imaginative writing can do this also but poetry is a form in which children can most easily describe and expand their feelings and perceptions.

Listening:
- Reflect on a visual you carry around in your head about a place you love. Or maybe it is a visual about a person you love, or a piece of music, or a delicacy of food. Write a short description of the memory.

Dialogue:
- What do you think about making a short poem from your memory you just described?

Action:
- Do it! Based on the memory you wrote about, make a poem, or write a song, if you are more inclined, and share with your class.
- Go back to Chapter 5, and reread the student teacher's planning for a problem-posing activity for preschoolers. Create your own problem-posing plan for kindergarten students.
- Investigate some children's books of poetry for kindergarten age group. Shel Silverstein is an author who is a favorite and many traditional nursery rhymes and poems have been set to beautifully illustrated books. Also, don't forget about the contributions of Dr. Seuss. Try out reading and discussing what you find with a five year old. Bring your results of "what happened" back to your class and in small groups brainstorm a way to develop a poetry unit for kindergarten learners.

Another teacher education student planned a problem-posing lesson using the children's book *La Isla* by Durros. She found success, doubt, and a myriad of learning opportunities as she did the lesson.

Listening:
- Listen to *La Isla*.

Dialogue:
- Engage the students in a discussion about how the story helps us with the understanding of a different culture through literature.

Action:
- Divide the class into four different centers:
  1. Blocks, the students will build their own version of la Isla
  2. Art—the students will use craypas to draw a picture as colorful as the illustrations in the book
  3. Math—the students will use cut-out shapes to make a "fruit salad" from which they will write out their own math problem

4. Writing the students will use the idea of flying over some place as the characters in the book do, to create a story of what New York City would look like from the air

(I will use minimal directions so as to allow the students freedom to interpret one aspect of the book in a creative manner. I will introduce the materials they will be using in Spanish. I have made note cards with the items (pencil, scissors, etc.) written in both English and Spanish, with a picture as well. After showing them these cards, they will become part of the classroom by being placed beside the place where the students find such materials. A short discussion after the book will serve to guide the students in their understanding and focus their thoughts. Some questions I might ask include: How would you describe the illustrations in the book? How do the girl and her grandmother "visit" the island? What are some places on the island that make it special?)

She wrote in her pre-planning:

The students are familiar with centers already, so they will be expected to follow directions. I have also used read alouds with the class before as a springboard for an activity to assess comprehension, so they should be prepared.

The children will be exposed to a culture and language different from their own through literature. They will put the book into a different context (through the centers) in order to deepen their understanding of the content of the story and make personal connections. They will use a specific aspect of the book in order to create something that is original and unique.

What Happened?

The lesson was comprised of two distinct parts: the listening and the action, which can be translated into the story and the centers. To me, the centers were to be the most important part of the lesson, because it was where the students had the opportunity to use their creativity as a means for understanding and developing the story. I was very glad to see that each student succeeded in doing this, in his/her own unique manner.

Surprisingly enough, the most difficult part of the lesson proved to be the reading of *La Isla*, even though I have read numerous stories aloud to the class. I had trouble holding the students' attention, which can be attributed to a variety of reasons, and may or may not have been my fault; I really am not sure. I used the same strategies as I normally do in order to focus the students, the most effective of which is making eye contact with the easily distracted students.

Although this was the least active and participatory portion of the lesson, it was, in many ways, the most crucial. The story was the basis of the centers, and comprehension of it was the main thing I was assessing, albeit through the centers. If the students could not remain focused throughout the story, then it would be impossible to assess their comprehension. I guess for these students, what I was assessing changed into being how they stay on talk, listen to directions, and keep themselves focused. (Much like the way that one's planned objects for a lesson might be changed midway through the lesson, assessment needs to be altered according to the way a lesson is going, which means it needs to be flexible.)

After I finished the story, I decided to change the discussion that I was planning on having, in order to ensure that the entire class had understood the basics behind the story. Usually any discussion I start after reading a book is meant to get the students thinking about what happened or about the characters in a way that leads to making connections to other books or to their own lives. I try to get them talking about a book at a more advanced level, rather than simply reiterating the story. But during this lesson, I asked much more specific questions in order to see who had been listening, and also to give all students a chance to know the story so that they could produce meaningful work during centers.

Ways of phrasing questions for students is something that I am still working on and this lesson gave me some practice. For a few of the students, in order to get them to say anything at all, I had to ask them "closed" questions; and afterwards S (her cooperating teacher) said I had done the right thing. A closed question is one that intentionally gears the student toward a specific answer, leaving them little freedom to think for her/himself. I learned, from being in this situation, that that is okay to do sometimes.

S. told me to write out the instructions for the centers on a big pad of paper. Since the activities have multiple parts, the students can start and then continue without having to worry about what to do next. It is good to let them get used to seeing the directions written out. S. told me that I needed to draw a picture for each one and that I should use different colors as well.

Phonics and Critical Literacy in Kindergarten

Back to our emphasis on critical literacy, one student observed a group of kindergarteners using critical literacy in a lesson that could also be categorized as a phonics and art activity.

An example of critical literacy in my current placement is when my class read Dr. Seuss's *There's a Wocket in My Pocket*. During the weeks before Dr. Seuss's birthday on March 2, the children began reading many books written by Dr. Seuss. In *There's a Wocket in My Pocket*, the phrases had rhyming words in them. Using these as examples, the teacher helped the students come up with their own phrases using rhyming words. For each item in the room, i.e. the shelf, calendar, the students thought up a monster that rhymes with that item. For example, for the calendar, one student came up with the monster named salendar. Then they put these words in phrases, i.e. "there is a salendar in the calendar." Moreover, the children used this interpretation of their literacy skills and transformed them into artistic skills and drew their particular monster. Therefore, the final product included a monster with a sentence strip attached to it which had a phrase such as "there is a salendar in the calendar" written on it. To further this critical literacy process, the teacher attached these creations to the actual calendar, chair, rug, etc., so that the students can see it everyday and enhance their reading, writing, and imaginative skills.

The issues of critical literacy and the contexts of kindergartners in our current world take us back to the language acquisition issues discussed in Chapter 2.

Listening:
- Write a few paragraphs about a situation when you didn't understand the language people were using to speak to you. How did you feel? How did you figure out what was going on?
- Read *I Hate English!* by Ellen Levine.

Dialogue:
- Discuss the story with a partner. Make connections between your personal stories and those of Mai in the book.

Action:
- Investigate various forms of technology and multimedia to extend activities in the classroom and to make connections with other people and children including World Wide Web and e-mail experiences.
- Read the following thoughts of a student teacher about these language issues:

I am a student teacher in a kindergarten class in the Bronx. The class is predominantly black and Hispanic. Six out of twenty-two students are English language learners. For 20 minutes each day they go for a small group session with an English as a Second Language teacher. The English as a Second Language teacher also serves a dual role as a recovery teacher. So there are many days out of the week theses students do not receive the literacy lessons they need. There is one student who has taken a liking to me. Her name is K. K. She has only been in this country for a month. She is originally from Santa Domingo. Due to the over crowding in the bilingual kindergarten class she is placed in this class where English is spoken all day.

I can understand some Spanish which is maybe why she comes to me. When she speaks to me in Spanish I'll answer her in English and she understands. She has told me in Spanish she doesn't want to speak English. I asked her why in English. She said because everyone wants her to speak it. I don't want her to feel forced to speak in English so we will keep the dialogue we presently have. When she is ready she will speak English. The cooperating teacher has requested a Spanish-speaking paraprofessional. K. doesn't' want to speak to the woman.

I told her the story of how they speak an African language in my home called Yuroba. I can understand the language but I don't feel comfortable speaking it. I think I sound funny. So, I only speak Yuroba round certain people. When I go to Africa, to Nigeria, maybe someone can help me. I am not as lucky as you are to have so many people to help with English. You're a lucky girl. She smiled and said in English, I am a lucky girl. I just smiled. It's only a matter of time.

Another teacher education student worried about using a story such as *I Hate English*.

I immediately thought of S. after the Read Aloud of *I Hate English!* I don't think that S. has an aversion to English, but I know that he is having difficulty learning the language. I wonder if books like *I Hate English!* would be helpful for him? I particularly thought that he might be able to speak more about his culture after the reading, thereby practicing his English in familiar territory. I worry that he might feel alienated after the reading though. Hence, my question in class about whether children might be singled out? Other children could speak about their own Asian backgrounds though, and non-Asian children could also talk about related experiences. Another concern is that S. is in Kindergarten, so he is not really well-versed in speaking about his background. I asked him once whether he spoke Cantonese or Mandarin, and he referred me to his Mom.

Nevertheless, the perspective in the book is very helpful to me as a future teacher. I definitely want to have a variety of books in the classroom, and read about a variety of experiences. It is also helpful to realize how difficult the transition to English is, and to try to help that be as comfortable as possible.

Another student talked about the children in her student teaching placement:

For a handful of my students, English is their second language. Being in a kindergarten class, where they are learning the fundamentals, I see it affects some in their learning more than others. Some have more confidence and have an easier time speaking English and picking up the concepts. They need more attention and one on one help.

Integrated Curriculum with Multicultural Stories: Where's the Math?

What about the other "parts" of an integrated curriculum? The science, math, art and history? Here are some suggestions:

Listening:
- What month were you born? Do you know any astrological information about your birthday month? Is the information from Greek history, Chinese history, African or South Asian history? Write a few thoughts about these questions in your journal.
- Read *Happy New Year* by Demi.

Dialogue:
- Discuss what your impressions were about marking time and seasons, art work, colors, designs and dragons, cooking, plants, dances and other aspects included in the book.

Action:
- Plan a way to ask questions about what children already know so that you may create child-centered, inquiry-based, mathematical learning environment based upon the multitude of facets of knowledge brought together in this storybook. How can children learn math concepts such as perceiving patterns, negotiating a sense of number, organize information, make inferences, and discover strategies for problem solving with activities you provide to coincide with this book? Devise a way to document children's use of the activities.
- As kindergarten children have subject area expectations put upon their learning, plan four learning centers or learning activities (i.e., science, art, social studies, literacy) that could be a spin-off from this storybook. What can you plan in terms of working with kindergartners and their parents as you use this storybook? Make sure your plans include ways to include and learn from various community members so that everyone involved can address deep culture as opposed to surface culture.

The previous thinking about integrations of art, science, math, and history lead us to be sure to point out the importance of music in any integrated curriculum.

Listening:
- Reflect on a situation in which you did not want to talk. For whatever reason, you wanted to use some other form of communication, which you did. Write about this.
- Read *Max Found Two Sticks* by Brian Pinkney (1997). New York: Aladdin Library.

Dialogue:
- Discuss what ways Max's story connects with your own. What about the setting illustrated here? Talk about that.

Action:
- Meet with a group of kindergarten students and together plan ways to make instruments for music-making.
- Using some of the suggestions from the children, make a problem-posing lesson for kindergarten students.

Another student teacher working with kindergarten and first grade students in the same classroom, reported her experience using problem-posing with multicultural literature. Her write-up of the experience combined her plan and what actually happened when she tried out her plan with a mixed-age group of kindergarten/first grade students.

The multi-cultural book I chose for this assignment is *Yoko's Paper Cranes*, by Rosemary Wells. The book is about a Japanese girl who learns how to make paper cranes from her grandparents. Later, Yoko moves to America and misses her grandparents. Then for her grandfather's birthday, she mails him a birthday card with three paper cranes. The grandparents hang the cranes by the windows during winter and think of Yoko every time they see them. I chose four students from my K-1 student teaching placement to participate in this activity.

Listening:
- I reminded the children of another Rosemary Wells book they had read called *Yoko*. I reminded them of the plot of the book, and then I asked if they remember the book and if they liked it. They made brief comments that they remembered and liked it "a little."
- I read *Yoko's Paper Cranes*

Dialogue:
- As I read the book the children became more enthusiastic, mostly due to the illustrations. The illustrations are very colorful and remind one of a collage made with paper of different patterns. The illustrations of Yoko's new home in California are surrounded by a border of American symbols like an American flag, watermelon, and ice cream cones. The children loved these illustrations. They made me stop reading so they could remark on how warm California looked, and how yummy the watermelon and ice cream looked. They also loved that some of the illustrations are shiny. They all wanted a chance to touch the book. One illustration shows a calendar with the date of Yoko's grandfather's birthday circled. They all then talked about when their birthdays are.

After I finished the story, I asked the children if they had friends or relatives who lived far away. The first grade girl spoke about her grandparents and cousins but couldn't remember where they lived. The kindergarten girl mentioned her grandparents who she says she has never met who live in Michigan. The first grade boy has friends in California and he described in detail, the plane trip he took when he visited them. The kindergarten boy spoke about his grandmother who lives in another country, but he forgot which one. I then introduced to the children that we would be writing letters to friends and family who live far away.

Action:
- Over the next week, I gave several mini-lessons on how to write a letter, and how to address an envelope. The children then wrote their letters, and decorated them using origami paper, like the illustrations in *Yoko's Paper Cranes*. I had sent a letter home to children's parents asking them to help the children choose somebody to write to. Three of the children wrote to their grandparents, and one child wrote to her cousin. Three of the children wrote in their letters messages like, "I love you," "I hope you are doing well," or "I hope to see you soon." One first grader wrote to his grandmother about how much fun he had over vacation when he was at her house. While they were decorating their letters, students made pictures of things that were special to them or the person they were writing to.

   Doing the activity in a small group was very important for these children. At their age and stage of development, it is important that they talk out loud to other children about what they are doing. It helps to clarify things for themselves. One kindergarten boy in the group is usually very quiet during class. However, the first grade boy helped to draw him in to the conversation. The first grader was talking to the children about how his grandmother has a lot of pets, and how her parrot is named, "Taco." This made the kindergarten boy (who loves animals) laugh, and then he started talking more about his own letter.

Regarding the dissonance between the push for subject area content knowledge and the need for the teacher to follow the interests, needs, and developmental contexts of individual children, another teacher education student wrote:

I've learned of the possibilities that many students are pushed too hard in Kindergarten, and as a result they experience a developmental lapse in 1st Grade. That literacy is a much bigger force that I ever imagined, and, at least in my classroom, literacy takes precedence over all else. And that although developmental differences are huge, and students can experience spurts and stalls of gigantic lengths, the average Kindergartener can blow you away with their breadth of knowledge, even if they don't express it.

Another student wrote:

> Something that happened where I learned a few things is when the class was discussing the research they did that day on their spring study. Specifically, one of the students said how he learned that all insects have six legs. Firstly, I did not know that so I definitely learned a new fact but more importantly it made me think about how intelligent children are and how so many people underestimate children and their abilities.
>
> Although they are so little they are like sponges and with the proper motivation and guidance they can learn so much! Many people consider kindergarten as the time to play and have fun but there are ways to accomplish that and teach them a whole lot at the same time.

References

Alarcón, F. (2001). *Iguanas in the snow and other winter poems/Iguanas en la nieve y otros poemas de invierno.* San Francisco: Children's Book Press.

Ajmera, M. & Ivanko, J. (1999). *To be a kid.* Watertown, MA: Charlesbridge Publishing.

Avery, C. (1998). *And with a light touch.* Portsmouth, NH: Heinemann.

Calkins, L. (1994). The art of teaching writing. Portsmouth, NH: Heinemann.

Demi (1999). *Happy new year.* New York: Dragonfly.

Durros, A. (1999). *La isla.* New York: Puffin.

Fox, Mem. *Whoever You Are.*

Graves. D. (1994). *A fresh look at writing.* Portsmouth, NH: Heinemann.

Lewin, T. (1990). *The day of Ahmed's secret.* New York: Mulberry.

Levine, E. (1995). *I hate English.* New York: Scholastic.

Pinkey, B. (1997). *Max found two sticks.* New York: Aladdin.

Polacco, P. (1998). *Chicken Sunday.* New York: Paper Star.

Porte, Barbara A. (2000). *Ma Jiang and the orange ants.* New York: Orchard Books.

Recorvits, H. (2003). *My name is Yoon.* New York: Frances Foster Books.

Seuss, Dr. (1974). *There's a wocket in my pocket.* New York: Random House.

Wells, R. (2001). *Yoko's paper cranes.* New York: Hyperion.

Winter, J. (1994). *Diego.* New York: Knopf.

Winter, J. (2002). *Frida.* New York: Levine.

· 7 ·

FIRST GRADE AND THE
LIGHT BULB GOING ON

*I remember a moment when reading really clicked for me. It was almost as if a light
bulb went on, illuminating my reading capabilities. It was the beginning of the first
grade and I remember sitting on the rug and the teacher was reading us a story . . . I
began to notice that I could read all the words. I remember going home to my mother
and telling her; I was so excited. I wanted read to her and my sister that night.*
TEACHER EDUCATION STUDENT

The first grade year is so monumental for children, their families and their teachers. Kindergarten was the bridge between the magical early childhood years in which pretend play, picture books, and bumpy peer negotiations (and lack thereof) are expected and acceptable. But now it's serious. This grade begins "real school." The grade level teachers in the higher grades sometimes tend to look down the hallways (and down their noses) if they see what they consider too much play, noise, peer interaction, and a lack of "academics." Often, the first grade teachers or the programs they implement, are blamed for students' lack of success in various areas that may surface in the later grades.

Ironically, for at least twenty years research (Goodlad, 1984) has documented the fact that schools that do promote play, noise, peer interaction, and integration of the arts in the academic curricula have students becoming successful achievers in all academic areas. Donald Graves, well-know literacy expert, spoke to principal, Shelley Harwayne, about her school, Manhattan New School; he said that the school "is a place that heals any sickness an educator might have. Walk in sick; walk out whole" (Harwayne, 1999, p. 3). She said that she understood his comments because there is a lot of smiling, laughing, hugging, conversing in many different languages all the time.

By using multicultural children's literature as a framework, first graders naturally go into learning with a depth and passion that makes the most of their potential. There is a growing consensus that the traditional scope and sequence approach to curriculum with its emphasis on drill and practice of isolated, academic skills does not reflect current knowledge of human learning and fails to produce students who possess the kind of higher-order thinking and problem-solving abilities we hope for. Past success in improving some of the basic skills in reading, writing, and math has not been matched by success in improving reading comprehension, writing fluency, or math problem-solving ability. In addition, it is evident that our schools are failing to produce future generations with even a working knowledge of the natural, physical, and social sciences, much less the kinds of minds that will create new knowledge and tackle complex problems in these areas. National professional organizations call for schooling to place greater emphasis on active, hands-on learning, conceptual learning that leads to understanding along with acquisition of basic skills, relevant learning experiences, and interactive teaching in a cooperative context. At the same time, these national organizations unanimously criticize rote memorization, drill and practice on isolated academic skills, teacher lecture, and repetitive seatwork.

Graves (1994) tells us, "When I observe first graders they are pouring drawings and words onto the paper with relentless fury. When they finish, they rush to the teacher to share their victory" (p. 3). Then he asks the clincher question, "What happens between first grade and the adult years? Children express themselves easily in first grade, but gradually they lose that creative freshness" (p. 3).

Carol Avery's son, who had visited her first grade classroom many times over many years said to her, "I don't get it Mom. I mean, what's the big deal? What you do's so simple." (Avery, 1993, p. 460). She reported that she felt like that was a compliment. She knew he was getting at the simple truth of first grade; the highly complex activities of being readers, writers, scientists, and mathematicians is much more intrinsically motivating than arbitrary lessons that have no connections with students' lives.

A student teacher wrote in her journal about what she had learned by student teaching in a first grade class:

> I have learned that 1st graders are much more capable and competent than I ever imagined them to be. I have learned that their writing abilities are amazing, and that through the lessons their teacher has for them, I learn more about myself, the world around me, and my own abilities than I did before. I have learned that math can be a whole lot of fun! I have learned that you can teach first graders math concepts that I thought would be sophisticated for fourth graders. I have

learned that some of the math concepts first graders are learning are very similar to the ones I learned last semester in a math class I took on the college level! I have learned that the books I remember reading, the books I used to love, are still loved by children, and that makes me happy. I have also learned that new books being written are great, and that I still love to read books meant for fourth or fifth graders. I have learned that these children seem much more independent to me than the special needs children I worked with for the last year and a half, and because of their differences I see them much more as little adults than "kids" and I find myself treating them as such. I have learned that respecting these students is a wonderful thing to do as a teacher.

I have learned to let go a little bit, learned that I cannot control everything and cannot force children to learn things I might expect them to pick up with ease. I have learned that it is so exciting when a child does learn something, and so much more exciting to see them do it on their own rather than have a teacher force feed it to them. I have learned that my moods and idiosyncrasies are always apparent to the students, and to always be aware that I am a role model. I have learned that students' moods can alter a teacher's, and usually the optimism and wonder of a child can make even the dourest situation, like a snowstorm in April, seem magical and fun. I have learned that I like first grade.

I have learned that working with struggling readers is not as hard as I thought it would be and not something for me to be afraid of. I have learned that while I respect and admire my cooperating teacher immensely I don't think I'll do everything exactly as she would. I have learned a little bit about who I am as a teacher and modifications I might make to suit me. I have learned that I can stand in front of a classroom, with 20 pairs of students' eyes and two pairs of adult eyes watching me, and teach a lesson proudly and confidently, and be heard and taught by those who are watching me. I have learned the importance of eating well and trying my best to sleep enough. I have learned that I really think I made the right decision going into teaching, and while it is more difficult and challenging than I ever imagined it would be, I love it more than I thought I would. And, perhaps most importantly, I have learned the value of invented spelling.

Invented Spelling

While invented spelling has been advocated for almost two decades by certain literacy specialist, some student teachers and parents are unfamiliar with the process and its importance in the developing writing process. One thoughtful teacher helped the parents of her students by having a special stamp made for her to use on student papers when they went home. The stamp said, "Invented Spelling Used Here." So, when a parent receives the writing of her first grader and it reads: [Bracketed interpretations weren't included.]

Dear Mom
I am a good Soodiet *[student]*
And I read a lot
I am good at silphkchul. *[self-control]*
I am in colors. I love you
And I hop you liked The APRIL
Fools.

She can praise and enjoy the writing with her son and not worry.

Considering the ambiguities of children's invented spelling and other aspects of emergent literacy, it is risk-taking teachers who expand learning environments of listening, speaking, reading and writing to include multilingual activities.

A student teacher planned such a problem-posing lesson with a chosen multicultural storybook. The book she chose for her lesson was *Magda's Tortillas (Las Tortillas de Magda)*. In our university class, we read and discussed some reviews of the storybook, some of which were positive, others of which were critical of the quality of the translation. In our process of problematizing, we discussed dialect differences in different geographical locations, and different vernacular ways of speaking in different communities. We reviewed a copy of *Are You My Mother?* by Dr. Seuss, which had been translated into Spanish. The publishing information revealed that the translation had been done in Spain. This accounted for the fact that some of the vocabulary words in the story were different from words used for the same items in Mexico and Cuba.

The student decided to keep her original plan to use the book and raised some of our questions with her cooperating teacher and the Spanish teacher at her school.

In this first grade class, some of the children are from Latin backgrounds and all of the children are learning Spanish in the school. Therefore, the teacher has chosen to use the book *Magda's Tortillas (Las Tortillas de Magda)*, by Becky Chavarria-Chairez, which is about a family's traditions of beginning to teach children to make tortillas on their seventh birthday. The teacher begins the lesson by introducing the concept of "rites of passage." This could include some examples from different cultures such as a Bar Mitzvah or Bat Mitzvah in the Jewish culture, driving, dating, or babysitting in the United States, or even going into Kindergarten.

Listening:
- The teacher begins by gathering the children in the meeting area of the classroom. She begins to talk with them about "rites of passage" in different cultures

and countries, perhaps even mentioning some from her own family to illustrate. Next, she begins to talk briefly about *Magda's Tortillas (Las Tortillas de Magda)*, explaining also that the text of the story is in Spanish and English.

Dialogue:
- The teacher invites the students to share some of the "rites of passage" in their own families, perhaps giving more examples from her own experience and other cultures or countries if necessary.

Action:
- The teacher would next invite the Spanish teacher, or perhaps a parent or community volunteer to come in to the class and read the story in Spanish, first explaining that the next day the story would be read in English.

Listening:
- Read the story in Spanish

Dialogue:
- What do you think the story is about? How do you know? What clues do you have?

Action:
- The teacher would then read the story to the class in English. Afterwards they would be asked to interview their parents, grandparents, or aunts and uncles or community friends about "rites of passage" in their families or cultures. They could present their findings and discoveries in a variety of formats such as showing artifacts in a presentation to the class writing a book, performing a play, or drawing a picture. In this way, they would have the opportunity share their family's traditional culture with the class and school communities in the format of their choice.

In my continual attempt to follow Willis (1995) guidelines of pushing our students to move beyond a neutral conception of culture in discussions of their relationship between schools and families and toward a better-defined conception of culture in a pluralistic, multicultural society, I introduce Mrs. Katz.

Listening:
- Try to remember and describe any stories from your childhood that involved a neighbor who was from a different background from your family, but became an extended family member. What brought you together? Was it an event, a person, an animal, a crisis, a happy time? Please write about the event and the person and their relationship with you.
- Read *Mrs. Katz and Tush* by Patricia Polacco

Dialogue:
- Discuss the relationship between Mrs. Katz and Larnel. How did they support each other? Connect any aspects of your writing previously with aspects of this story.

Action:
- Research the history of a tradition or a celebration in your family? Where did it originate? In your journal write or draw a past/present "snapshot" of a tradition in your family.
- Write about a story which has been retold in your family or in a group of your friends. How has this story changed during its retelling? What are the underlying meanings or truth in this story? What have your family members or friends learned from it over the years? Create a way to show this information to your class.
- Communicate through a letter, a telephone call, an e-mail, or a personal conversation with a family member. Explain your memory that you wrote about and get a response of your accuracy from that family member. Bring your reports to the next class meeting for discussion.

Based on thoughts about family influences on our daily lives, and the "bigger picture" idea of thinking about activist ways to be more of a "human family," several students became very excited about the potential of the storybook, *Sam y el Dinero de la Suerte / Sam and the Lucky Money* by Chinn.

One student decided to create a problem-posing plan based on a two-way bilingual classroom of first graders. She decided to begin her lesson with the Action section.

Action:
- I would start out with the action in order to really get children involved in the topic and to gain a background for the topic we are discussing. The action I chose was a neighborhood walk. Having the students walk through Chinatown and really get an opportunity to talk to vendors or storeowners on the street. Children are given cameras to take pictures of interesting sites along the way, as it would be difficult for first graders to take notes.

Dialogue:
- As soon as we return to the classroom, discussion is important to get some ideas from the trip going and to share with the rest of the class specific conversations that others may not have heard on the walk. The conversation could be opened with likes/dislikes about the trip where everyone can share and then more specific questions can be raised based on the comments made by kids or questions they have for each other.

Listening:
- The story is read in both the English and Spanish languages, with children listening to the story in both languages regardless of the native language. Students are then asked to share their feelings about Sam's experience and to talk about things in the book that we saw in our walk or what things are different.

Another student teacher who was working in a school in Chinatown, saw firsthand the power of story, language and shared meaning, and friendship and respect. Based on her experiences, she choice to make the following problem-posing plan.

I chose the book *Story of the Chinese Zodiac* retold by Monica Chang to get these children interested in learning English (and teaching me Mandarin and Cantonese). I thought I would incorporate something personal, like their zodiac sign, and something cultural, like their specific Chinese zodiac sign along with something we could share from our respective cultures.

This story is especially helpful for the class I'm in because it is presented in a bilingual English/Chinese format, and features some of the most amazing illustrations by Arthur Lee.

The book tells the story of a great race which determines which animals get to be part of the Chinese zodiac. A central character in the tale is the Rat, who hatches a cunning plot and is in my opinion the most interesting character. There are some really memorable scenes as well as well-written, simply put, characters with amazing pictures to draw children right into the story.

Listening:
- After reading the book aloud in English and having had each child read the book to one another in pairs, in Chinese and English, I have a one on one with each child and ask who their favorite character in the story was and why. Sort of like an oral book report.
- Then when I get the class back together as a large group, I ask the children if they know anything about the Western zodiac and proceed to tell them the various signs and symbols of the Western zodiac.

Action:
- In the back of the room on a bulletin board I would post huge pictures of the symbols of the Western zodiac and the animals of the Eastern zodiac. We would go around in a circle and each tell the class our Chinese zodiac sign and try to figure out our Western zodiac sign. Then each child will write, on huge post-it paper, the symbol for their sign in Mandarin or Cantonese and in English and post them next to the pictures on the back board. Assuming there are many children born in the same year, I may only have two different animals covered in the Chinese zodiac. So then I would ask the children if they will

help me draw and post symbols and words for the remaining characters. Hopefully they won't say no.

Dialogue:
- When that is done, I ask the children to think of questions they might have about the story or either of the different zodiac characters. After that I would ask them if they could write a story about the Western zodiac and its characters which they would be and why.

Action:
- For homework they write down which Western zodiac symbol they would be in a short (one-page) story about how their chosen sign for the Western zodiac was chosen to be a part of the whole zodiac family.
- The next day in class we split up into groups by the zodiac sign we've chosen for our chapter of the story. Each group designates one artist and one editor; the rest of the group is writers for their chapter of the zodiac.
- At the end of the unit, we put together all the chapters for the "Story of the Western zodiac," which I will get bound and printed and have sent home with the children to save or give to their parents who they can read their story to in Mandarin / Cantonese and English!

Environments in First Grade

We talked about early childhood learning environments when we discussed younger children. The early childhood learning environment is every bit as important with first graders too. The ideas of Progressive Education in the early part of the twentieth century and the work of John Dewey taught us much about environments in education. *Progressivism* was a movement that advocated the application of human and material resources to improve the American's quality of life as an individual. In terms of education, progressive ideals demanded that the needs and interests of students rather than of teachers should be the focus of all learning in schools. Students were responsible for maximizing their potential with the teacher as a facilitator.

Listening:
- Write about an experience you have had with a "progressive" educational experience. Refer to any of the many works available by John Dewey, or other progressive educators, if you need to refresh your memory.
- Research the life and work of Lucy Sprague Mitchell. She was a progressive educator in Chicago and an acquaintance, colleague, and occasional

collaborator with John Dewey. She is most noted for her work in neighborhood early childhood programs actually putting into practice progressive ideas. Think about why it might be that she is not as well known as John Dewey as you collect information. Report your findings to your class.

- Read Dr. Anne Sullivan's (Sullivan, in Quintero & Rummel, 2003) introduction to her found poems:

> These . . . found poems, constructed from the text of John Dewey's *School and Society*, bring into focus some of the critical themes of the book by distilling Dewey's prose and shaping it in ways that heighten attention to key concepts. In constructing these poems, the poet maintained these rules for herself: 1) I cannot add words of my own; 2) I cannot change meaning; 3) I may re-order words or sentences if meaning is not altered; 4) I may change verb endings (drop or add an *-ed, -ing, -s*); 5) I may alter and add punctuation. The resulting poems are proposed as strategies for bringing students, and others who may be intimidated by or uncomfortable with Dewey's prose, into relation with his work. They are invitations, doorways, beginnings.

- Read the following found poems and write personal insights and inferences you can make about John Dewey as you read.

Found Poems from John Dewey's School and Society
by Anne McCrary Sullivan

Mathematical Problem

There is just so much desirable knowledge.
There are just so many needed accomplishments

in the world. Then comes the mathematical problem	**On School**
of dividing this by the six, twelve, or sixteen years	To
	School
of school. Now give the children every year	
just the proportionate fraction of the total;	rigidly set
by the time they have finished	give
they will have mastered the whole,	a shock. (p. 15)

covering so much ground during this hour
or day or week or year. Everything comes out

perfectly at the end—provided
the children have not forgotten, provided
the children have not forgotten (p. 33).

Learning

Here is a certain disorder
and chairs—artistic, hygienic,

There is not silence.
Persons are not engaged

in maintaining fixed
physical postures.

Their arms are not folded.
They are not holding
their books
thus and so.

There is confusion, the bustle
of doing things to produce results

and there is born a discipline
of its own kind and type.

The only training
that becomes intuition

Is that got through life itself (p. 17).

Reference

Dewey, J. (1920/1990). *The school and society.* Chicago: University of Chicago Press.

Dialogue:
- Discuss the poems and how they inform you about Dewey's work and other aspects of progressive education.

Action:
- Read more about the work of Lucy Sprague Mitchell. One source is a biography by Joyce Antler (1987), *Lucy Sprague Mitchell: The Making of a Modern Woman*. Create a found poem, based on her work and words, using Anne Sullivan's guidelines mentioned in the Listening Section.
- Choose one essay or chapter of a book from an educator whom you admire and write one or more found poems about that person's work. Bring your poems to share with your class.
- Write about the environment in the classroom in which you are student teaching. What aspects seem to be recommended by educators you have been studying? What aspects are different? Respond in writing.

One student wrote about the environment in her student teaching placement:

The books talk about how important it is to expose children to books, classroom writings, and so on at a level they can see and utilize. I also remember the alphabet stuck on my desk as a child. If the alphabet in my student teaching classroom was moved lower or to any place more accessible, I think it would make a huge difference in the students' willingness to work harder.

Another issue that I have in the classroom is the word wall. The teacher does refer to it and she does ask the students to find the word on the word wall when they don't know how to spell something. The only problem is the design of the word wall. Although it's spaced out across the chalk board, the words are so small that the students can't see from their seats. Then when they need a word, the must walk across the classroom, take the word off the wall and bring it to their desks. It takes up way too much time and it gets in the way of other kids who need the word. It's kind of silly to have an alphabet in a classroom that students can't even use.

Dewey and Sprague Mitchell and other educators have always encouraged the importance of supports in the learning environment—both physical supports such as accessible word walls and many books available, and the idea of emotional supports.

Poetry, and the vibrant art work in many multicultural children's books, can help teachers provide these needed supports for children.

Listening:
• Write about a memory of a friend or classmate being kind to you in a situation when you were sad or afraid. What happened to you? What were you feeling? How did the other person approach you? How did this make you feel?

Dialogue:
• Discuss creating a poem with your written memories.

Action:
• Observe a first grade classroom working on a poetry unit. What seems to be the most enjoyable for children? Document what you see and what evidence you see of the children's literacy development.
• Research topic of teachers working with children surrounding difficult issues. Visit the Rethinking Schools Web site at rethinkingschools.org. The organization has several insightful articles about this topic. Report to your class about what you find.
• Read the following journal reflection by a student teacher who had been working with a child on her poetry.

I was working with my student, Sara, sometime last month, editing her poetry. This whole semester, the students had been working on poetry and writing their own poems as they learned different techniques. At first it was shape poems, and then poems based on feelings. Most recently it was learning to use adjectives in their poems as well as incorporating onomatopoeia. After all those weeks, the students were now in the process of choosing their favorite poems and editing them for compilation into their own poetry books. I was helping Sara edit.

One of the parts of editing was for the student to circle words that looked funny to them. In this way, the teacher wasn't just stepping in and forcing the student to correct everything, but it was allowing the students to identify their own areas of need. I was in the process of going over these words with Sara. For me, I always vacillate in these types of situations: do I just tell the student the correct spelling, make them look up the word, or help them sound it/spell it out. In this case, I asked her an open-ended question, "Sara, what's one way I can figure out the correct spelling for this word?" Instead of just asking me to spell it for her, she replied, "Use a dictionary."

After she lugged the dictionary over and was methodically flipping the pages, I just happened to ask her how she knew how to use the dictionary. - Plenty of her peers were averse to utilizing this big book and many of them were still unfamiliar as to how to find something once it was in their possession. Sara answered me simply, "You showed me." I was pleasantly surprised. I didn't even remember when I had done that. However, I felt so privileged to have been a part of this student's knowledge acquisition process. From this incident I learned that you don't always realize your own impact on a child's learning life. Any moment can be a teachable moment that opens up a whole new world of understanding and knowing for a child.

Reflecting More on Language Acquisition and Multiliteracies in First Grade

Language acquisition of multilingual learners is still at the forefront with this age group too. A group of teacher education students in their first semester of course work read "Bilingual Children's Mother Tongue: Why Is It Important for Education?" by Jim Cummins at the University of Toronto (http://www.iteachilearn.com/cummins/mother.htm) and had a small group discussion. Their initial impressions reveal glimpses of how important this information is for all teachers, not just teachers who are planning to teach English Language Learners. They were asked then to write their own most striking first impression and that of a member of their group.

D: "I found the most important statement is that destruction of language is counter-productive. This is a multilingual world and being multilingual should be highly valued. I learned that C. is bilingual and was struck by the fact that knowing two languages makes you a better student in both. P. was surprised that becoming stronger in your mother tongue can make you stronger in school language. She said, 'For me personally, what struck me most about the article was when it talked about "the level of development of children's mother tongue is a strong predictor of their second language development.' Since I was speaking Slovak before English, this was a surprise because ironically, they say 'don't promote the mother tongue because the child won't learn English,' but in my case the opposite was true. I always excelled at English and it is and always has been my favorite subject." (We—faculty member and bilingual adult student—talked and I said I suspected that her family was so wonderful at providing rich language interactions and opportunities in her mother tongue that she was ready with her strong foundation of language acquisition to go to school and acquire English joyfully, with no problems.)

A. agrees that linguistic experience in the home is a foundation we must build on and every child has a right to have their talents promoted and recognized. You must consider the child's background. "Children's cultural and linguistic experience in the home is the foundation of their future learning and we must build on that foundation rather than undermine it."

T. said "I enjoyed the article by Cummins. I am bilingual and while I've always enjoyed it, I never realized the importance of it. The author emphasized how proficiency in a mother language is not detrimental to learning English but actually very important because it is an interdependent process. Furthermore, it is so important to ensure that children do not lose their mother language while in school and while learning a new language because it could result in cultural isolation. Key is the analysis that rejection of a child's mother language in school is rejection of the child. The article highlighted many of the advantages of bilinguals in an increasingly globalized world, and these were the points I felt to be most important and salient to my life.

Another student wrote further in a personal written response to several articles on Cummins' website:

I read about language and power issues and the inequalities in power distribution in multicultural classrooms in the United States. I learned that the impact of such homogeneous methods is astounding and potentially catastrophic in a child's growth and development. I'm glad I read these articles because I will be that much more aware and be better prepared to acknowledge and address the concerns for my future students, whereas previously I didn't even realize how ostracized a person can feel just by the use of one language over another.

And another wrote:

> The article reminded me of myself as a student and that I should not focus on my ethnicity nor should I try to hide my ethnicity. Cummins feels that encouraging the diversity in each child can only add to the success within the classroom. Cummins states children are pressured to appear the same as their peers. Diversity instead should be portrayed as a natural element of life and the classroom.

Critical Literacy in First Grade

In Chapter 2, when problem-posing was explained at length, it was emphasized that this problem-posing, often described as critical pedagogy, combines reflective thinking, information gathering, collaborative decision making, and personal learning choices. I repeat that this is important, again, because the approach allows students to move beyond a neutral conception of culture in discussions of their relationship between schools and families and toward a better-defined conception of culture in a pluralistic, multicultural society (Willis, 1995). A problem-posing format using children's literature, especially multicultural children's literature, encourages collaboration and enhances multidirectional participatory learning. In other words, in this context, learning not only is transmitted from teacher to students, but teachers learn from students, and students learn from each other. Problem-posing helps us find ways to look at alternative ways of knowing and people's real experiences and real achievements.

Listening:
- Think of a symbol (a visual of some sort) that has a special meaning for you. Draw a sketch of it and write a few lines about the meaning it has for you.
- Write about any knowledge you have about the origins of your own name. Write about your family's discussions and feelings about the significance of names. Who chose the names of the babies in the family? How were the names chosen? Did you have any ceremony attached to the naming? What about nicknames? How did they come about? Write what you can remember. (Yes, older students and adults are just as interested in naming as young children.)
- Read *A Boy Called Slow: The True Story of Sitting Bull* by Joseph Brucac.

Dialogue:
- Did anyone in your group know this story? What have you heard about American Indian naming ceremonies and traditions? In what ways did any of your naming stories have any similarities with this story?

Action:

- Read the following plan a group of student teachers wrote when considering the use of this story, especially at the beginning of a school year when it is important to establish community in the classroom:

Listening:
- First it is important that we establish a learner centered environment. The students will sit in a semicircle and we will read the story and then ask them think about inventing a name for themselves. We will then ask them to disperse around the room to write about the names they have created.

Dialogue:
- Then each student will present their papers to a partner. This activity will help students form bonds and make sense of each other as members of a community.

Action:
- The students will create a way to present the meaning behind the names of the partner and develop an artistic way to present this for the mural the class creates. This activity gives students the opportunity to learn about American Indians, themselves and each other. This is intended to encourage student talk, build community, and consider meaningful story.
- Read . . . *If Your Name Was Changed at Ellis Island* by Ellen Levine (1993). The book is written for children and is a historical explanation of what Ellis Island was, who came there and why, and some of the procedures and policies that immigrants were exposed to when they arrived.

It is always important to keep an open mind regarding what we are all learning and as Donaldo Macedo (1995) always reminds us, we must always ask what is really going on here? This is true in terms of policy and politics and it is true in terms of the multicultural children's literature we use in our classrooms. For example, when a teacher education student found the storybook, *Knots on a Counting Rope* by Bill Martin Jr. and John Archambault, we were all happy to see the beautiful book and have the opportunity to further our knowledge of American Indian people.

The story is about an American Indian boy and his grandfather. The boy is blind and his grandfather tells him the story of when he was born and how his family discovered that he was blind. The grandfather's story helps the boy to deal with his blindness. The grandfather uses a counting rope and adds a knot to it for each time he tells the story—when the rope is filled the boy will know the story by heart. The grandfather tells the boy that he does this because he will not always be here to tell the boy himself.

In addition, the story seemed to be a way into information sessions with children about issues of ability and disability, potential and barriers. Then we found an article by a Navajo scholar and learned about inaccuracies in the book. She and her collaborator explain that Ted Rand's illustrations suggest primarily that the story is set in the Navajo nation, but his pictures show a mix of material culture from other different nations as well. For example, traditional Navajo men in the story have a variety of hairstyles of the Atsina, Blackfeet, Mandan, and Piegan nations. Also, Pueblo people are shown at a horse race wearing traditional ceremonial clothing that would be inappropriate for such an occasion (Reese & Caldwell-Wood, 1997). Whereas, these inconsistent details may seem insignificant, they are very important in terms of critical literacy and the importance of history.

So, should the book be totally censored and never used? I feel not. I feel it is a good way to engage first grade students in critical literacy and a starting point for them to learn to be critical researchers.

Finally, first grade is an opportune time to stress to learners the potential in learning from the arts.

Listening:
- Write or draw about anyone in your family or group of close friends who plays a musical instrument or plays in a band, or sings in a chorus.
- Listen to an example of jazz, blues, classical, hip-hop, folk, and religious music.
- Read *Music, Music for Everyone* by Vera Williams.

Dialogue:
- Discuss what is going on with the page borders and the illustrations. Are the borders similar on the music-filled pages? Discuss the diversity of ethnic groups and ages of people represented at the party. Discuss your feelings about music and its importance to family, community, and school.

Action:
- Interview family members and friends about the role of music in their lives. Report your findings to your class.
- Investigate musical instruments from other countries and cultures. Bring recordings or pictures back to class to share.
- Review the following Web sites for information about young children and music.
  http://makingmusic.net
  http:www.childrensmusic.org

- Review the following Web site for information about Waldorf Education which has a strong music component.
  http://www.fortnet.org/rsws/waldorf/faq.html#6
- Research an article or book by Tom Barone, Elliott Eisner, or another art educator you have learned about. Find an artistic way to present your information to the class.
- Research the history of playwright August Wilson. He uses the history of jazz as a frame for presenting the history of African American people in the past century. Choose a play to read in it's entirety. Plan a way to share some of what you have learned from August Wilson with first graders and share your plans with your class.

In an interview, Bill Moyers (1995), asked Quincy Troupe, "How did jazz and blues influence your poetry?" (p. 417). Troupe answered:

> They shaped it in very important ways because both jazz and blues have distinct languages and, of all the cultural contributions that the United States has made to the world, those two have been the most profound. The blues is constructed close to the way Americans, and especially African Americans from the Midwest and the South, speak. We tend to speak in circles—we come back to say things over and over again, just for emphasis—and there you have the whole repetition of lines coming back like refrains. Jazz, on the other hand, can be notated . . . Jazz provides the model for taking a text and improvising on it in a performance. . . ." (p. 417)

Problem-posing with children's literature provides a model for learning and leaves room for improvisation by the learners.

References

Alarcón, Francisco X. (1999). *Angels ride bikes and other fall poems/Los ángeles andan en bicicleta y otros poemas de otoño*. San Francisco: Children's Book Press.

Antler, J. (1987). *Lucy Sprague Mitchell: The making of a modern woman*. Princeton, NJ: Yale University Press.

Avery, C. (1993). *. . . And with a light touch: Learning about reading, writing and teaching with first graders*. Portsmouth, NH: Heinemann.

Brucac, J. (1998). *A boy called slow: The true story of Sitting Bull*. New York: Scott Foresman.

Chang, M. (1994). *Story of the Chinese zodiac*. San Francisco: Pan Asian Publications.

Chavarria-Chairez, B. (2000). *Magda's tortillas / Las tortillas de Magda*. Houston, TX: Arte Publico Press.

Chinn, K. (1997). *Sam and the lucky money*. New York: Lee & Low Books.

Chinn, K. (2003). *Sam y el Dinero de la Suerte / Sam and the lucky money*. New York: Lee & Low Books

Chinn, K (2002). *Xiaoshan di ya shui qian/Sam and the luck money*. New York: Lee & Low Books.

Cummins, J. http://www.iteachilearn.com/cummins/mother.htm.

Goodlad, J. (1984). *A place called school: Promise for the future*. New York: McGraw-Hill Trade.

Graves, Donald H. (1994). *A fresh look at writing*. Portsmouth, NH: Heinemann.

Harwayne, S. (1999). *Going public: Priorities & practice at The Manhattan New School*. Portsmouth, NH: Heinemann.

Moyers, B. (1995). *The language of life: A festival of poets*. New York: Doubleday.

Polacco, P. (1992). *Mrs. Katz and Tush*. New York: Bantum.

Reese, D. & Caldwell-Wood, N. 1997). Native Americans in children's literature. In Violet J. Harris (Ed), *Using multiethnic literature in the K-8 classroom*. (pp. 155–192). Norwood, MA: Christopher-Gordon.

· 8 ·

SECOND GRADE:
WHAT IS REALLY IMPORTANT?

Many curriculum textbooks list the strategies of importance in terms of curriculum for second grade in terms of methodologies such as book time, sharing, math, writer's workshop, reading, library, projects, music, and choice. I have chosen once again to quote a student teacher's journal so that these strategies can be seen through the eyes of a new teacher. Then, my students and I will illustrate how these strategies may be used to address of topics of importance to the children and their learning.

A Student Teacher's Overview

The second grade classroom is the center for literacy "children learn the oral language through exposure," J., my cooperating teacher states. In order to foster a literate environment it is important to make children excited about reading. Children will enjoy reading if they understand the dynamics of reading. "Only part of our library is split up into reading levels, that way the kids don't feel labeled." Having only part of the library labeled enables the students to have freedom within their choices. They know that the red bin holds their "just right" books, but they can feel free to try to read any of the books. It is discouraging for children to see that they are on a lower reading level. It sets them apart from their peers and a feeling of inadequacy will diminish their desire to progress.

"It is important to model what the children should be doing in their reading." Modeling is incorporated within Read Aloud. It is in Read Aloud that J. exhibits reading techniques. To help them learn reading recall, J. will say, "We haven't read this book in a while and I am having a little trouble remembering what happened." He will then read a paragraph from selected pages, he will look at the pictures, and he will read the "blurb" on the back of the book. This shows the children how to recall what they have read when going back to a book. Some of the other topics that I have witnessed during Read Aloud were character description and dialogue. With dialogue the questions that were raised were, "How do we know when someone is talking" and "How do we know who is talking." This was a guided discussion with the entire class, resulting in very perceptive comments made by the students. When the children go to their independent reading, they take with them different reading techniques that they are eager to implement.

"Each year a teacher sets a focus and this year I really wanted the focus to be on Reading and Writing." That focus is clearly visible. Read Aloud, Independent Reading, and Writing are fit into the larger morning block. This allows the children to take the time that they need to finish their book or get started on writing out their new idea. Writing is an important adjunct to reading. Although the writing process is arduous, the children are motivated by the end result, the publishing stage. The stages of writing are mapped out in chart form:

I have an idea

I am working on my first draft

I am getting more ideas for my first draft

I am editing my work

I am publishing

Each time the children progress to the next stage, they are eager to move their name along the path to publishing. "I like the chart, because it always keeps them writing. Once they finish and publish their work, they know that they have to keep going."

It is during Independent Reading or Writing that J. conferences with different students. "I watch the kids, first, because you can tell a lot from behavior. The kids that I see having a difficulty are the ones that I generally try to conference with." Some of the behaviors that signal that a child is not understanding what they are reading are flipping through the pages, not recalling the story, or misbehaving. During a typical conference, J. will ask the student to read to him. Through the student reading aloud, J. will determine if the problem is reading comprehension, word decoding, or possibly that the book is above the student's reading level. These teacher/student conferences are essential for the student. Everyone will have a conference with J. so that the children do not feel different and their peers will not question their reading ability. Writing conferences work in the same way. However, there are more conferences with the children who are already finished with their first draft. This is critical in getting the children to write more. Within their How-To Books the children had a hard time writing more than a list for their first drafts. It was only when J. separated the list and asked, "Why?" for each stage that the children understood that explanation was key. The point was well understood by the students, because their papers were filled with explanation about each step. "Look at his paper. That is how you know that they got."

For almost three decades, numerous researchers including Donald Graves (1983, 1994), Donald Murray (1985, 1990), and Lucy Calkins (1994) have focused on the writing workshop as an alternative to traditional writing instruction, as a learning environment that fosters learning in ways that transform the social context of the classroom. The writing workshop, along with a number of other reading and writing pedagogies, including whole language, language for learning and writing across the curriculum, reader-response theory and writing process movement, falls under what John Willinsky (1990) termed "The New Literacy."

The New Literacy consists of those strategies in the teaching of reading and writing that attempt to shift the control of literacy from the teacher to the student; literacy is promoted in such programs as a social process with language that can from the very beginning extend the students' range of meaning and connection (Willinsky, 1990, p. 8). It is this enhancement of meaning and connection that I believe we are building upon by using problem-posing with children's literature.

Critical Literacy and Passion

So, considering literacy as a social process with language that can extend the students' range of meaning and connection, I would like to raise the issue of passion as it relates to critical literacy, multicultural literature and the understandings it can foster. I always ask students early in their teacher education experience to think and write about what they are passionate about. I go on to show, with their illustrations of passion, that these passions can often be the basis of meaningful teaching and learning. For example, I am inspired every time I read about J.R.R. Tolkien's passions *in From a Letter by J.R.R. Tolkien to Milton Walman, 1951*:

> But an equally basic passion of mine (in congruent with Linguistic aesthetics) *ab initio* was for myth (not allegory!) and for fairy-story, and above all for heroic legend on the brink of fairy-tale and history, of which there is far too little in the world (accessible to me) for my appetite. I was an undergraduate before thought and experience revealed to me that these were not divergent interests—opposite poles of science and romance—but integrally related . . . (pp. x–xi)

He goes on:

> . . . I dislike Allegory—the conscious and intentional allegory—yet any attempt to explain the purport of myth or fairytale must use allegorical language . . . (xii–xiii)

And then, for me, he connects history, art, reality and dreams:

> After all, I believe that legends and myths are largely made of "truth," and indeed present aspects of it that can only be received in this mode; and long ago certain truths and modes of this kind were discovered and must always reappear. (p. xvi)

I am inspired by these "heady" ideas, and I feel they can come alive through literature and problem-posing. For example a teacher in Minnesota, has been using fairy tales and legends with her elementary aged students (in grades 1, 2, and 3) for several years. I use her work to introduce the practicality of lesson like these to my students.

Listening:
- When you were a young child, what was your favorite fairy tale or folktale? Do you have any idea why you especially liked the story? What did the story teach? What beliefs were represented by the story? Please write about your memories.
- Listen to Ann Green explain some teaching activities using fairy tales:

> I started my reading program by teaching through genre. After I introduced a genre to my class, the students would read and respond to literature that fit into that genre. I would meet with them in small groups two to three times a week to ensure comprehension and to discuss what they were reading. I would culminate each unit with a project that would allow the students to demonstrate what they had learned about the genre. My students wrote fiction, poetry, and fairy tale books. They wrote biography reports and created puppets of their characters; they made historical fiction mobiles, and performed mystery skits.
>
> Our fairy tale unit was a class favorite. To prepare for the unit I gathered as many different versions of the Cinderella story possible. These stories came from a variety of different countries and cultures. I introduced the unit by asking the students what they already knew about fairy tales. We made a list on the board. Their ideas were very limited to what they'd seen in Disney movies and books. I then gave the students a compare and contrast chart. For the next several days the students read the Cinderella stories in pairs. After each book they had to fill in the following categories on their chart: title, country/culture, main character, evil characters, magic person or objects, and the reward. When the charts were complete, we made a class list of the elements found in all of the fairy tales the students read.
>
> The students then wrote their own Cinderella tales based on the list of elements.

1. The story starts with, "Once upon a time" or a similar phrase.
2. Magic events, characters, and objects are part of the story.
3. At least one character is wicked or evil.
4. At least one character is good.
5. There is usually someone of royalty involved.
6. The main character always gets a reward in the end (goodness is rewarded).
7. The story ends with, "They lived happily ever after."

(Green, 2003, in Quintero & Rummel, pp. 85–88)

Dialogue:
• Please discuss in small groups: What were your memories of fairy tales? What were the "truths" underlying the tales? What ways are gender and family roles portrayed? If you were rewriting this tale, how would you change it?

Action:
• In small groups follow Ms. Green's class Elements of Fairy Tales list and discuss and create a group tale: Share your group's tale with the whole class.
• Find versions of the Cinderella story from at least five different cultures. What are the underlying teachings about women in these stories? Compare traditional Cinderella stories with stories in contemporary media with a Cinderella theme such as the films *An Officer and a Gentleman* or *Pretty Woman*. How is the underlying message of Cinderella stories presented to girls in the media? Present your findings to the class.

A student teacher became passionate about pursuing legend along with multilingual lessons with her second graders.

This lesson is designed to incorporate Spanish into the classroom. Many parents and children speak Spanish at home or in their Spanish speaking community. Spanish is similar to English in the way that some words sound, and how they are spelled, therefore, this lesson is designed so children make connections between the two languages.

Listening:
• Does anyone here have parents who speak another language other than English? Do any of you speak another language, probably the same language as your parents? What languages do you speak? If you don't speak another language, what are some other languages that you have heard, or that you know of that are different from English? A lot of answers will be discussed, and it will be very likely that one child will say Spanish. This will provoke the discussion about Spanish.

- Ask the Spanish speaking children, or the children of Spanish speaking parents where their parents where born, and where they were born? Some children might be familiar with South America. Use a map to aid in this discussion.
- Then ask one of the Spanish speaking parents to come in and read the book called *The Llama's Secret*, by Argenina Palacios. This book is a Peruvian rendition of the Great Flood Story, in which a llama warns the people and animals to seek shelter on Huillcacato to avoid the rising sea, Mamcocha. The parent is going to read the Spanish edition of the book.

Dialogue:
- Where did this story take place? What is this story about? What did you notice about the Spanish language that you didn't already know? Would any of the Spanish speaking children like to share something with the class about what they might have learned from the story? What did the Llama do in the story?

Action:
- Now the teacher will discuss the follow-up activity, with the aid of the Spanish speaking children, and the Spanish speaking parent(s) in the classroom, and a variety of Spanish books, and Spanish dictionaries.
- Children can write down words and make connections with Spanish and English by making a list of connections. The words might be spelled completely differently, but the children are able to make connections by the context of the story, the Spanish dictionary, or help from the other children in the classroom.

Other follow-up Actions:
- Do a lesson on folk tales. How do folk tales provide us with history? Incorporate *The Llama's Secret* in this discussion.
- Do linguistic activities, including other languages in the classroom. How are they similar or different from each other?
- Read the book in English and observe what the children notice. Make sure that both editions, Spanish and English, are in the classroom for the children to look at and read.

Another student took to heart the focus on personal memories, passions, and story.

Listening:
- I will gather the students and have them sit in a circle. I will begin by telling them a story that my parents told me when I was a little girl. I will tell them a story they might be familiar with, such as *Hansel and Gretel*. Then, I will explain how scared this story made me. Stories like this are told to children to

keep them from wandering off. In fact, many different cultures have popular stories about evil beings that will steal misbehaving children.

Dialogue:
- I will ask the class a series of questions. What stories were you told as a little child to keep you from wandering off? Do you know of any other stories like this? The students will share their personal experiences with the class.

Action:
- The teacher will assign each student to read a book called *Baba Yaga: A Russian Folktale*. The story is about a little girl who lives in Russia. Her mother died and her father married a wicked woman. One day, the little girl's stepmother told her to get certain materials from her step aunt. Her step aunt was a Baba Yaga, an evil woman who ate people. Before going to her step aunt, the little girl went to visit her mother's sister. She explained to the little girl how to escape from the Baba Yaga. She would have to feed the dogs so that they wouldn't attack her. She would have to feed the cats, so that they wouldn't scratch her eyes out. And, she would have to tie a ribbon around the tree so that it wouldn't poke her eye out. The little girl went to the Baba Yaga, did exactly what her aunt told her to do, and got away safely. But, when the Baba Yaga heard that she got away, she punished her animals and stomped on her tree. In response, the animals and the tree explained that they let her go because she was nice to them. When the little girl returned home, she told her father what her stepmother put her through and he banished her immediately.

Dialogue:
- What did you think of this story? Did you think it was scary? Would it prevent you from wandering off? Different cultures have different way of expressing the same concern. There is a shared desire among various cultures to protect their children. *Baba Yaga* is one example that is commonly used in Russia. Just like I said before, "Hansel and Gretel" is popular in the United States. In Germany a popular story is "the Berchta." From Japan there is "Obake/ghost" and "Oni/Devil." Do any of these stories sound familiar?

Action:
- Each student will be required to write a story that is reflective of their culture and what they believe would help keep children in line. The content of each story should reveal the answers to the following questions? What character did you invent and from what culture did your character come? What parts of that culture did you include? The students will be encouraged to use all the elements of story (setting, plot, crisis, resolution). Then, the students will be given the opportunity to form groups of four and choose one story to act out. Each group will get a chance to present, while the rest of the class evaluates how effective that story might be in keeping children in line.

Another teacher education student became interested in the ancient histories and legends of her culture and explored lesson possibilities with *How the Sea Began: A Taino Myth* retold by George Crespo.

Listening:
• To begin, I would read aloud to my students *How the Sea Began: A Taino Myth*. This book uses a myth to explain how the sea was developed in Puerto Rico. Through beautiful illustrations and storytelling, this myth gave one explanation of how the sea was formed.

Dialogue:
• After the reading, I would have a group discussion about the specific myth in the book and then lead the children into a discussion about myths. First, we would work together to define what a myth was. We then would discuss myths we have heard in the past. Finally, to lead up to the activity, I would lead a group discussion of questions about nature that they are curious about. I would start with an example: "What are some reasons that could possible explain why the sky is blue?"

Action:
• After reading about and defining myths, I would have the students work in small groups to write their own myths. First, they would have to choose what question they would want to answer and then collaborate on a story. I would encourage them to work together to use their imaginations to explain an everyday thing in nature. Each group would create a book to represent their myth. Just like the one we read together, they would put together their own book with the written story and the illustrations. We would then keep these books in the class library.

   I would continue with this activity and have the groups plan a play based on their myth to share with the class. Therefore, the myths could be shared with the other students in a dramatic way.
• Finally, if I wanted to take this activity one step further, I would explain to the children that many cultures and religions have their own myths to help explain things in the world, just like the Taino culture did. I would encourage the children to go home and interview their parents to see if there were any special myths in their own cultures. Hopefully, the next day the students would be able to come back and share these myths with the class!

Passion about Our Worlds

A student teacher who is very passionate about using the world that she and her students live in chose the storybook, *Madlenka* by Peter Sis. The story is about a little girl named Madlenka whose tooth is loose. She visits her friends and neighbors around her block to let them know. We are introduced to each of them and learn a little about their culture, language and customs. The illustrations are vivid and display different symbols, monuments and geographic locations that are representative of the countries mentioned in the book. In the beginning of the book there is a map of Manhattan that shows exactly where Madlenka lives, and at the end of the book there is a map of the world, showing the locations of countries of the people that she interacts with without even leaving her city. The student teacher deliberately begins her problem-posing with the Dialogue section.

Dialogue:
- How many of you were born in a country outside the U.S.? Or how many of your parents or grandparents were born somewhere else?
- What are some ways you can learn about different cultures and people? Besides traveling miles and miles away, couldn't you just walk down the street in your neighborhood? There are many different people in this city that speak different languages, dress differently and eat different foods. (Between 120 to 140 languages are spoken in New York City alone)
- If there are students from other countries, having a map and marking the country would be helpful to the class just to give them an idea of how much diversity there is in the world as well as the classroom.

Listening:
- Read *Madlenka* to class out loud.

Dialogue:
- What kinds of things is Madlenka exposed to? What does she see and learn about from her friends? Mark the countries that her friends/neighbors are from on the map.

Action:
- Have a guest from another country visit the class. Prepare the students first by telling them a little about the guest and to think and write down questions that they would like to ask the guest. For example, if you were Madlenka and could ask any of her neighbors some questions, what would you ask? Have some extra copies of the book so the students could look through them.
- After the visit and with the questions the students have, get them ready to interview someone that they know. It could be a relative, neighbor, classmate, or friend. Send a letter home to guardians because they need to be accompanied by someone. The interview could be taped or written down but students must be prepared to share with class.

Another student who is passionate about travel and using travel as a way to learn more about people and the world chose a book about travel and Baghdad.

The multicultural storybook used is called *The House of Wisdom* by Florence Parry Heide and Judith Heide Gilliland. The book is about a boy, Ishaq who seeks to become a scholar and travel the world in search of books for a famous library in Baghdad. He travels to many countries and learns much about different cultures and languages.

Listening:
- The teacher will begin the lesson by reading the book to the class. The teacher will also have a map of the world posted adjacent to the reading area. After reading the book, the teacher will ask the students to recall the cities Ishaq visited, making note of the cities on the map.

Dialogue:
- In groups of four the children will discuss/write/or draw about the countries they have traveled to or wish to travel to.

Action:
- In class:
  The class will be set with stations that represent a different country. Each group of four will sit at each station and be able to look over material on that specific country, i.e., maps, pictures . . . Each group will speak to the class about that country and what they found interesting or surprising.
- Out of class:
  Each student will interview parent/relative/friend who had traveled to another country or traveled to the U.S. from another country. The students will share their interviews in class the next day.

It is important to remember that while our varied places in the wide world are important, our small, personal worlds within our families are important too. Adoption is an issue that involves feelings and information at all ages. Another student teacher planned this lesson, in part, because she fell in love with the storybook, and in part because she saw similar situations among some of the children in her school.

The storybook *Allison* by Allen Say talks about a young Japanese girl named Allison, who is adopted by a wonderful couple in the United States. One day while looking in the mirror Allison realizes that she looks more like her doll than her parents. At that moment, she begins to question her adoptive parents and demands to see her biological parents. Later on in the story, Allison comes to terms with this discovery with the help of a stray cat. The student wrote:

In my second grade class, we have four centers; a library, art center, listening center and a computer center. In the library center, I would have various books about Japan's culture and traditions in a separate bin. As a homework assignment, I would ask every child in the class to visit a Public Library and to borrow a book about Japan. I would encourage them to read it at home and to record a daily journal entry about their reading. In the art center, I would have their kimono paintings hung up. In the listening center, I would have all their favorite dolls or toys along with some Japanese audiotapes. Last but not least in the computer center, I would have them type an article describing a family activity done at home.

Listening:
• I would wear a kimono dress and ask if someone knew where it was made. I would ask them to describe their kimono paintings. I would show the book *Allison* and ask them to make predictions. I would read the story.

Dialogue:
• What kind of a present did Allison get? Why did she feel disappointed when she looked in the mirror with her mother and father smiling over her shoulders? How did she act after knowing the truth?

Action:
• I would explain activities at the various centers.

Another student teacher has a passion about gender roles in families, in schools, and in larger contexts. She planned the following activity based on her passions.

The class would start out by listening to a read-aloud of the book *Players in Pigtails* by Shana Corey, and of course would interject, share, offer opinions, ask questions, and participate in other various ways during the read-aloud in order to remain engaged, active, and able to form relevant connections between the book and their own lives.

Listening:
• Katie Casey loves baseball so much that she decides to play even though her parents aren't too sure about it. Is there anything that you love as much as Katie Casey loves baseball? (The kids can discuss this topic freely and write about it in their reading journals.) How would you feel if people made fun of you because of what you love to do or told you that you couldn't do this anymore?

Dialogue:
• What do you think of the fact that Katie loves baseball? What about other girls who like sports or video games? How about boys who like dancing or playing with dolls?

- Is it okay for boys to have long hair? Girls to have short hair? . . . girls to wear pants? . . .boys to wear dresses?. . .girls to wear the color blue? . . . boys to wear the color pink?. . .boys to play on a girls' softball team? . . . girls to play on a boys' football team? . . .two friends who are girls to hold hands? . . . two boys to hold hands?

   (Allow the children to freely discuss and debate their answers, and go off on tangents and share anecdotes. Let the kids run their own discussion, and only step in and mediate or share your own opinion when you think it's absolutely necessary. The underlying question will likely be something like, "Why are some of these things okay, but others are not?"—questioning the basis and origination of double standards.

- What would you do if you saw a new (and very nice) boy on the playground, playing quietly by himself with a doll? Would you talk to him? Laugh about him with your friends? Make fun of him to his face? What would other kids do? (I would encourage the children to be totally honest—nothing they say is wrong, or bad, or will make me angry. Everything is fair ground and totally okay to say during this discussion . . . of course at the beginning of the year I would have established a policy of honesty, respect, and confidentiality during discussions in our classroom).

Action:
- Katie Casey and the other girls who played baseball were laughed at by the people in the stands because they were different. Create a short skit to perform in front of the class. The skit should involve someone who is getting made fun of, or teased, or ignored, or excluded based on how they look, what they like to do or wear, where they are from, their height, their weight, etc., and the skit should also include your idea of what you would do in order to help this person. For example, you could create a skit about a boy who gets made fun of for wearing glasses, and as a solution you could have a fellow classmate step in and (verbally) defend the boy against the bullies, or the boy could speak up for himself, or the boy could go to a teacher and tell him/her what's going on . . . it's up to you. Show me how you think that the problem would be best resolved.
- Give the children the writing topic "If a woman was the president . . ." and give them total free reign . . . let them write about whatever they think would be different about the world if the president of the United States was a woman.
- Oftentimes throughout history, men who make a difference in the world were studied very closely, celebrated, and even made famous, while many women who made differences in the world went unrecognized. Do some research in the library and pick a woman from any time period who made some type of difference in this world. Write a report, draw a picture, or make a poster or diorama that tells/illustrates who this woman is and/or what she did to make a difference.

Other:

* (Somewhat long-term:) We could read the book *Harriet the Spy* every day as a class during read-aloud time and then watch the movie as a class. I think that this movie is an excellent one for everyone to watch, and it depicts wonderfully the point that you should do whatever's in your heart, even if people who are close to you, such as your best friends and your parents, don't understand why you do it or even disapprove. Gully says to Harriet at one point during the movie something to the effect of, "You are your own person. That scares people. And it's going to keep scaring people all throughout your life. You just need to stay true to Harriet and everything else will work itself out." I think that the children will form connections between the book, the movie, and the gender problem-posing activity on their own. Later on we could do the same thing with the book and movie *Matilda* (by Roald Dahl). Many discussions and reading journal entries would be included during (and following) the read-aloud sessions (maybe we could read a chapter a day, but of course that depends on the kids and the discussions that develop as a result of the reading).

The Brink of History

Back to Tolkien's idea that legend (or story) lives on the brink of history, I stress to students that our study of history must be ongoing. What does history mean when studying curriculum and learning? Critical literacy is a process of both reading history (the world) and creating history (what do you believe is important?). No one develops or learns out of the context of family, community, country, or world at the present time or without a connection to the past—the stories of those who have gone before.

This book has been making the case that curriculum and learning develop among particularities, among persons and objects in families and communities. Large sweeps of history take meaning from the small stories.

The history of the Armenian peoples provide an example of this. Their survival owes much to their attachment to their native language with its distinct alphabet although the largest Armenian community in the world today is in the United States. For 1700 unbroken years they have expressed the beliefs at the heart of their identity through text illuminated with art. For hundreds of years manuscripts were illuminated, embellished with luminous color with either literal or symbolic decoration to help with the layout or reading. In modern times this oneness of the written with the visual was lost except in books for children or more recently in conceptual art. The written and visual are moving together again in this new graphic age and so literacy has to be intertextual. A literate person must be able to read between and within these different texts. Writing is central to this intertextual literacy. "Writing is not just a mopping up activity at the end or a research project . . . (it) is also a way of knowing . . . a method of inquiry" (Richardson, 1994, p. 516).

Listening:
- Write about a memory you may have of your parents or a family member helping someone who was in danger. What do you remember about what was going on? As a child, how did you find out about this?
- Write about what you know about life among different nationalities and ethnicities of people in the decade before the Civil War.
- Write about a job you had as a young child that helped to contribute to your family's livelihood. How did you feel about this job and how did other members of your family and community feel about your work?
- Read *The Lost Village of Central Park* by Hope Lourie Killcoyne.

Dialogue:
- In small groups, first discuss any of your group members' knowledge about life among different groups of people in the 1950s. Now, discuss your examples of a family member's helping someone in a difficult situation and your memories about working as a child.
- Now discuss the story *The Lost Village of Central Park*. What was old information? What was new information? How did your stories from the discussion above relate to anything in the story?

Action:
- Research both primary source and secondary source documents about Seneca Village. Report your findings to your class.
- Research slave narratives about the Underground Railroad and other ways people gave sanctuary to runaway slaves. Report your findings to your class.
- Research the situation of poor families from Ireland who came to the United States and Canada. Where did many families settle? Why? Who helped them? How did they survive? Report your findings to your class.
- Visit one or more museums and document ways oppressed peoples' histories are documented through art. Report, using a visual medium, to your class.
- Read *Aunt Harriet's Railroad in the Sky* by Faith Ringold and plan a problem-posing activity to share with second graders.
- Read *The Poisonwood Bible* by Barbara Kinsolver (1998). Kingsolver's character Orleanna in *The Poisonwood* Bible states:

I was occupied so entirely by each day, I felt detached from anything so large as a month or a year. History didn't cross my mind. Now it does. Now I know, whatever your burdens, to hold yourself apart from the lot of more powerful men is an illusion. (p. 323)

What does this quotation and this story have to do with early childhood learning? Report to your class.

- Read *The Watsons Go to Birmingham—1963* by C.P. Curtis. This story is about a family from Flint, Michigan who travel to visit a grandmother in Birmingham, Alabama. They find themselves in the middle of some of the most chilling moments in the struggle for civil rights in the 1960s. This is a wonderful novel, full of history, that second graders will love. Plan a way to use it with students and share your plans with your class.

Autobiographical Influences

A student teacher is passionate about Spain, Spanish music, and flamenco dancing. Her passion is reflected here.

Listening:
- After reading the book, *The Story Dance* by Barbara Satterfield, the instructor will review what an heirloom is. Afterwards, the instructor will share his/her own heirloom (in the case of this particular project I happen to have my grandmother's manton, castanets, hair comb, and pin that she wore when she danced). The teacher may opt to play flamenco music and explain that flamenco tells a story. In most cases, the stories are sad and are about someone's broken heart.
- Review any words that students may have had difficulty with.

Dialogue/Journal Entries:
- Ask students if they know of any heirlooms that are in their family. Ask students if they can think of any types of music that are similar to flamenco. Ask students if they have anything that they would like to pass down to future generations. If their ancestors could have left them anything from the past, what would they have liked to have and why? Could students relate to any of the characters or experiences in this book?

Action/Homework:
- Have students ask their parents if they have any family heirlooms. If students have family heirlooms, ask students to draw them and to be prepared to share the Who, What When, Where, and Why, and Hows about their heirloom(s).

Specifically, the class would be interested in knowing where the heirloom came from (what culture).

- Have students draw the item that they would like to pass down and to be prepared to share it with the class.
- Students will build a time capsule (shoebox or a box large enough to place the drawings and explanations of items from previous work and will put their heirlooms away for the next generation—next year's class. When this unit comes up next year, the instructor can share the class's heirlooms with the new students and continue the tradition.

Another student based her problem-posing on a book her two young nephews were passionate about. *The Drums of Noto Hanto* by J. Alison James is a story about the people of the village of Noto Hanto. In 1576, in Nabune, a village on the Noto Hanto peninsula in Japan, the people cleverly scare away their attacking enemy using drums and masks made of bark and seaweed. This is one of those stories which is exciting for children and rich for more study of history, geography, government, art, and legend.

Listening:
- Read *The Drums of Noto Hanto.*

Dialogue:
- After reading the book, I will use the pictures and begin a discussion with the students "What is happening here? Who are these people? Where are they? What is a samurai? Where is he going? What do the people in the village do? Why did they use the drums? What kinds of noises does a drum make? Why did they use masks? What kinds of masks are they?"

Action:
- After discussing the book the student will then create their own masks. Masks can be made by dipping strips of newspaper into wheatpaste and covering half of a round balloon in layers. Once it is dry the balloon can be popped and the mask can then be painted. While the mask is drying, students will collect things to decorate their masks with. Once the masks have been finished, we will act out the story of *The Drums of Noto Hanto* using our masks and some pots as drums.

Integrated Curriculum

In any discussion of curriculum, I find it is important to remind students of people in history who combined science, math, music, art and literature as whole, in terms of both enjoying the world and learning from the world. Here Mitsumasa Anno helps me.

Listening:

- Think about a figure in history who has studied and taught us who have come later through an integration of art, science, music, math and literature. You might be reminded of Frida Kahlo, Isaac Newton, Marie Curie, Leonardo da Vinci, Bach or Bethoven. You might think of someone that is not as well-known. Write what you remember about this person's work.
- Read *Anno's Journey* by Mitsumasa Anno. This is a wordless storybook with artwork clearly intended for asthetic appreciation and integrated learning. In this book, the traveler begins his trek alone, buys a horse and rides through progressively more populated scenes with both literary and artistic allusions, and the simple acts of children playing or a mother touching her baby. Much of human experience and emotion is contained in small details—children despairing after a lost balloon, flirting lovers, a mother touching her child, and in this particular book, historical landmarks of Europe are illustrated.

Dialogue:

- What did you see? What memories were evoked for you? What sorts of historical documentation were included that made you want to revisit some previous learning?

Action:

- Read all of Anno's work that you can access. Some classics are: *Anno's Mysterious Multiplying Jar, Anno's Magic Seeds, Anno's USA*. Plan a problem-posing lesson for second graders based on Anno's work.

Another resource I enjoy using with teacher education students and young children which opens up huge possibility for the integration of the arts is *I Live in Music*.

Listening:

- Think of setting in which you are immersed in music and visual art. Write about the setting, the event, the feelings and thoughts you have when you are there.
- Read *I Live in Music* by Ntozake Shange and Romare Bearden.

Dialogue:

- How did the poem about music and the artwork in the book connect with some of your personal experiences? What questions do you have about this type of integrated learning?

Action:
- Investigate *Life Doesn't Frighten Me* by Maya Angelou with paintings by Jean-Michel Basquiat, *may i feel said he*, poem by e.e. cummings with paintings by Marc Chagall, and *Dance Me to the End of Love*, poem by Leonard Cohen paintings by Henri Matisse.
- Plan a problem-posing lesson for second graders using this integration of the arts. Report to your class.

A Student Teacher Using Problem-posing with Second Graders

In Chapter 6, a student teacher used the storybook, *Isla* by Durros. Here a student used it with second graders. This shows once again that the multicultural children's literature can be used with different grade levels and ages. The intellectual teacher (Giroux, 1988) who observes the students well and trusts their strengths can facilitate these.

At the school where I am student teaching, the second grade class theme study for the year is the history of New York. The students just finished a section on immigration. The focus of my problem-posing lesson further explores this concept.

Listening:
- I begin by saying "I know a few of you have immigrated here, to the U.S., from another country. By a show of hands, let's see who you are. Does anybody have parents who have immigrated to this country? Raise your hands. I have to raise my hand too because my parents came from Europe. How about grandparents? Does anyone have grandparents or great-grandparents that have immigrated here? Or does anyone know neighbors or friends who are immigrants (remember your friends in class count)? What about immigrants we don't know personally? Who are some immigrants that are in the news or on T.V. or in the movies?" (I will allow a few children to respond after each question.)
- Then I explain, "The grandmother of the girl in the story I am going to read is an immigrant, and she tells her grandchild about her homeland. The storybook is *La Isla* by Arthur Dorros. Some of you may be familiar with another of his books, *Abuela* (show them). Isla is a sequel to that book, which means it's like part two of the book."
- I read *La Isla*.

Dialogue:
- A discussion will be held revolving around these questions:

In this story, how did the little girl come to appreciate the homeland of her grandmother? What are the kinds of things that we found about La Isla? If we wanted to find out about the homeland of immigrants we know or even about the homeland of people we don't know but would like to know about, what kind of things would you like to find out? (List responses on chart paper.)

Action:

- I will then ask the children to partner up and interview each other about homeland or the homeland of someone they know. I say that if they don't want to share, they don't have to; they can listen in another's interview. I remind them to look to the chart that we made up here for ideas for your questions. Try and ask about at least two things. (I give example of if I were interviewing L., I might ask him about the kinds of places there are to visit in the Dominican Republic and what kinds of foods there are.) I explain that after your interviews we will come back as a group and share some things that we learned. Then we will have time to draw some pictures. For the pictures draw (or write) something about your homeland or the homeland of someone you know. If you can't think of anything to draw, you can draw something about your homeland here in New York. Remember, immigrants have two homelands, the homeland of the country they moved from and the homeland of where they live now.

What Happened? (Excerpts from Student Journal)

Isla was a hit. Although the lesson did not go exactly according to plan, the outcome was better than expected. Students were very engaged. My personal belief as to why this lesson was successful is related to its interactive design. Because students took an active role in the experience from the beginning, for each student, personal meaning was given the concepts behind the lesson.

Each part of the lesson allowed students to take initiative and develop the details. During the reading, we stopped at points where interest was high or at points where questions arose and held a brief discussion. After the reading, students were able to brainstorm a long list of things they could find out about another's homeland. Some items included what the place looks like, what kinds stores there are, what kinds of things there are to do and what kinds of things people wear. After the brain storming session, students used the list to interview each other. Then, time was given for the students to draw.

Originally, I had intended to hand out interview worksheets to the students to guide their thinking. Because of time constraints (only fifteen minutes was allotted for interview time), I changed my plan at the last minute and decided to ask the students to interview each other without a planned worksheet. The interviews went well. The students did not follow the directions exactly, but the basic concept of learning about the homeland of others was accomplished. There was a steady flow of conversation and the children enjoyed talking about themselves and their families.

The only other part of the lesson that did not turn out as I expected is related to the extension activity. I had hoped that more students would draw a picture of their native homelands, but because I gave the choice of drawing New York, a majority of the children drew New York. Even so, I would not change the lesson design if I had a chance to do it again. I did not want students to get hung up on figuring out what to draw—I wanted them to enjoy the experience while making a concrete representation of what a homeland means to them. This, I believe, was accomplished.

I don't want this to sound all poshy and prettied up, but truthfully, the lesson went well. The students were able to extend on their theme study (related to immigration to New York), learn about a number of different countries and develop an appreciation of the differences among them. When I have a chance to implement this sort of lesson in my own classroom, I will probably follow the same approach, as well as implement the original lesson I had intended (Where the students would interview a person outside the classroom and conduct a mini-research of that person's homeland.)

What One Student Learned about Teaching in Second Grade

What I've learned about 2nd grade is that it's a time of a lot of great learning, especially at my school. The children are exposed to numerous concepts and terminology that I never heard of or learned until perhaps middle school. Because of the new constructivist philosophy to teaching, no longer is there the graduated, portioning out approach to dispensing knowledge. As young as second grade, students are being introduced to mathematical concepts, like symmetry, and literary techniques, like onomatopoeia. The amazing thing you'll find too about today's kids is that often they've heard of these things or have some idea about these "grown-up-like" terms. Students are full of their own background knowledge and often are ready and excited to incorporate what they already know with what they are learning in class. During one of my math lessons on symmetry, one of my students cut out something and told me it was a symmetrical moustache; what great imaginations they have, as well!

Something else I learned about second grade is that it's never too early to have children in your classroom with problems. In my class I have students with emotional, behavioral, visual, fine motor, and academic problems. It's quite new to me to know that children these days come to school with such a host of things hindering them from learning; it's actually quite sad sometimes to know all the strikes that are against your students. Second graders still want to get hugs from their teachers. They still will draw pictures for you and tell you they love you. Second grade girls still have their own little sagas of who is friends with whom. They get mad at each other and make up with one another, laugh one minute and cry the next on a routine basis. Second grade is a really interesting place!

First of all, since this is my first placement, I learned the importance of being a reflective practitioner. The value of going back over a lesson I just conducted and figuring out what worked and what didn't is immeasurable . . . it's the only way I can continue to develop and move forward as an effective teacher. Second, I learned that with young children, you must be very specific and detailed when giving instructions, directions, etc. . . . I have mostly worked with older kids and it took some time for me remember to explain all my instructions very precisely and specifically for my 7–8 year olds.

Finally, I learned that consistent rules, expectations and routines help to foster a smoother functioning classroom. Kids don't fare well with the unexpected—they like consistency, routine, and what to expect. Making sure the kids know what the plan for the day is, what the rules about everything are, and what they can expect in most situations keeps the classroom running smoothly with fewer disruptions.

References

Calkins, L. L.M. (1994). *The art of teaching writing*. Portsmouth, NH: Heinemann.

Corey, S. (2003). *Players in pigtails*. New York: Scholastic.

Crespo, G. (1993). *How the sea began: A Taino myth*. New York: Clarion.

Curtis, C. P. (1997). *The Watsons Go to Birmingham—1963*. New York: Bantum.

Durros, A. (1999). *La Isla*. New York: Puffin.

Giroux, H. (1988). *Teachers as intellectuals: Toward a critical pedagogy of learning*. Critical studies in education series. Granby, Mass.: Bergin & Garvey.

Graves, D.(1983). *Writing: Teachers and children at work*. Portsmouth, NH: Heinemann.

Graves, D. (1994). *A fresh look at writing*. Portsmouth, NH: Heinemann.

Heide, Florence P. & Gillialand, Judith H. (1999). *The House of Wisdom*. New York: Mulberry Books.

James, J. Alison (1999). *The drums of Noto Hanto*. New York: DK Publishing.

Killcoyne, Hope L. (1999). *The lost village of Central Park*. New York: Silver Moon Press.

Kimmel, E. (1991). *Baba Yaga: A Russian folktale*. New York: Harper House, 1991

Kingsolver, B. (1998). *The Poisonwood bible*. New York: HarperCollins.

Levine, E. (1992). *. . . If your name was changed at Ellis Island*. New York: Scholastic.

Murray, D. (1985). *A writer teaches writing*. Boston: Houghton Mifflin.

Palacios, A. (1996). *The llama's secret*. New York: Troll Associates.

Richardson (1994) Richardson, L. (1994). Writing, a method of inquiry. In N. Denzin and Y. Lincoln (Eds.) *Handbook of qualitative research* (pp. 516–529). Thousand Oaks, CA: Sage.

Say, A. (1997). *Allison*. New York: HoughtonMifflin.

Sis, P. (2000). *Madlenka*. New York: Frances Foster Books.

Shange, N. & Bearden, R. (1999). *I live in music.* New York: Welcome Enterprises.

Tolkien, J.R.R. (1977). From a letter by J.R.R. Tolkien to Milton Waldman, 1951. In Tolkien, C. (Ed.). *The Silmarillion*, pp. x–xxiv. London: HarperCollins.

Willinsky, J. (1990). *The new literacy: Redefining reading and writing in the schools.* New York: Routledge.

·9·

JUST NEW BEGINNINGS

*I believe all of us come from more than one community and also benefit from that,
. . . I have a different story to tell and if people are serious about communication, we
have to hear other people's story . . . I'm doing this for a little girl somewhere in the
middle of America with fuzzy hair and yellow skin, who will see my name and the
power of an Eastern name that is not Osama bin Laden or Saddam Hussein.*
SUHEIR HAMMAD, 2003

This book has described a journey about hearing other people's stories.
When we truly listen, there are no endings, just new beginnings. It is
my continuing journey and a continuing journey by teacher educators and their students in schools all over the country. The ongoing qualitative
study reveals findings of our using problem-posing activities with literature
and continues the dialogue about integrated curriculum for early childhood
education. The data has been analyzed by categories dictated by the theoretical perspectives of a post-formal theory, critical theory, feminist theory, autobiographical narrative, and by the target learning areas of critical literacy,
multicultural children's literature and integrated early childhood curricula.
The analysis of the data has supported the belief that in order to support critical early childhood education, we must look at various fields of study and various forms of lived experience and local knowledge as recorded through the
arts, media, and all aspects of children's work. So what does this really mean
for early childhood teachers?

Just today, I heard a neonatologist speak about his work and he commented
about how some of the same ethical and moral issues that he and his colleagues
are faced with in medicine are similar to the ethical and moral issues that educators face on a daily basis. We got to a point in the discussion in which "big
picture" issues were being addressed, and he said, "I read somewhere about a
group of second graders not reading at 'grade level.' Who gives a damn? Are

the kids happy? Do they eat well? Do they feel good about themselves? Are they loved?" I agree that these should be our issues. And I believe the data collected with the help of teachers, students, and young children mentioned in this book show that problem-posing using multicultural literature is an effective way to address both the big questions and little questions.

It is clear from my words, the topics I have chosen to include in this book, and the examples of student work included that I hope to encourage, inspire, and even nag, educators to be activists with and for young children and their families. Children and families come to education with knowledge and information and glorious strengths. Kincheloe (2000) reminds us that marginalized peoples make up localized power groups who typically produce popular forms of knowledge. These knowledge forms are powerful. They can be drawn upon for psychic protection from often dangerous ideological teachings of the power bloc of people who do not value these particular forms of knowledge. I believe that by using problem-posing in ways just touched upon here in these few pages, educators can potentially begin a powerful revolution in terms of the construction of and respect for many more "knowledges" than are now available to most of us.

One class of my teacher education students read an interview with Miles Horton and Paulo Freire (1990) from *You Make the Road by Walking*. The information and ensuing discussion raised their consciousness a notch or two regarding the big issues involved in curriculum and education. One student reflected:

> . . . we strive toward the democratic ideal, applying it whenever we can as the premier form of governance. Freire, here in his interview, applies it towards curriculum organization. He says, "the more people participate in the process of their own education, the more the people participate in the process of defining what kind of production to produce, and for what and why." While it is vitally important for us to make sense of our own education, education first needs to make sense to us. For what purpose are we learning? Admittedly, I personally cannot say that I fully understood the magnitude of the significance and importance that education played in my own life until only very recently. I never did see the bigger picture. The curriculum I experienced in my own educational career felt very segmented. Rather than understanding how my social studies curriculum was structured and its intentions, I simply went along for the ride not remembering where I started, nor knowing where I was headed. Needless to say, I have vague memories of even the path that was taken. A fish that swims in the sea cannot see that vastness of the sea in which it swims.

Another student wrote:

> After reading what Paulo Freire said about democracy in education, I couldn't help but think about the teacher that I am currently working with at PS 158. I

agree with Freire when he says that students' participation in the curriculum is important in achieving democracy and development. My teacher exemplifies this in her classroom. Although the periods of the day are defined in terms such as word study or writing workshop, the children have a choice in what individual activity, game, or worksheet they want to do within that topic. She feels that allowing them to participate in choosing the activities they do helps them to be more interested in the material, learn decision making, and helps them to be more productive. I see the children excited about and learn from what they do throughout the day and I believe it is because they are taking part in choosing and creating these activities.

Mary Catherine Bateson (2000) also addresses ideals and freedom:

> Freedom reveals the underlying differences and allows them to develop. . . . A rapidly changing world requires improvisation as we find ourselves onstage without a script, perhaps with grace, perhaps in awkwardness and anger. (p. 15)

I believe that a way for us to facilitate evolving scripts for our "stage" is to use lived experience, science, legend, the arts and history—all possible in children's literature—for real participatory learning. We can learn from each other and be energized by hope.

> Wisdom, then, is born of the overlapping of lives, the resonance between stories. . . . Hope for a sustainable future depends on reshaping the life cycle— not the individual life cycle alone but the overlapping and intersecting cycles of individuals and generations, reaffirming both the past and the future, not only in families but in the institutions we build and share. (Bateson, 2000, p. 242–243)

The way I see it, is that never before has there been such an urgent need for educators to ask questions that have never before been asked, to children, about children, and for children—for all of us. Steinberg and Kincheloe (2001) remind us that

> . . . comments and analysis changes our orientation to multicultural education in that we study not only the effects of oppression on the oppressed but its impact on the privileged as well. . . . It does mean that we see all human beings shaped by race, class, and general inscriptions of power. Indeed, part of what we would define as a characteristic of a critically educated person is conscientiousness of the way power dynamics of race, class, gender, and other social dynamics have operated to help produce one's identity and consciousness. (Steinberg & Kincheloe, 2001, p. 26)

This has been shown through the work of the teachers and student teachers who have shared ideas in this book. This is hard work; this is many teachers' life work.

A teacher in St. Paul, Minnesota said:

> You have to both show what you're going to do with students and you have to show what has come before. I've tried over the years to find out as much as I can about my students' lives, their culture, as well as what their interests are — whether it's cartoon shows, whether it's watching Nature on PBS and using that information as a "hook," as reinforcement, as a motivator to the kids. And if I start it then the kids build on each other and then I gain more information too, so I never know how a lesson will go when I start out with that frame . . . but that's what makes teaching fun for me — with those conversations I have with the kids: I never know where they're going to go! I can teach the material many times, many different years, material that's always successful, but I have no idea what will happen in those conversations and that keeps it fresh. (Boehlke, 1998)

Another trusted friend and literacy specialist working diligently with brilliant students in one of the poorest, most threatened schools in Brooklyn, New York gave advice to educators:

> Base your teaching on experience. Be passionate about what you do and bring that passion to the children and keep it going. Be a lifelong learner and learn from the children. Take chances, take risks. Share. Bring the outside world into the classroom. . . . Be grounded in your skills, be grounded in your curriculum, but don't just stay with that one book — be open to other resources. (Russell, 1999)

Steinberg (2001) laments that

> . . . Great people, humanitarians, are ignored in favor of many, louder voices, or privilege of color or class. We demand a pedagogical revolution. Voices from teachers and students that will rise up and demand social justice and curricular inclusion of broad global perspectives. (p. xxiv)

I believe children and their teachers, who experience problem-posing curriculum with the glory of story can fuel this revolution.

Universal	Espiral
Spiral	**universal**
there are	no hay
no endings	finales
just new	sólo nuevos
beginnings	principios

Francisco X. Alarcón (1997)

References

Alarcón, Francisco X. (1997). *Laughing tomatoes and other spring poems/ Jitomates risueños y otros poemas de primavera*. San Francisco: Children's Book Press.

Bateson, Mary C. (2000). *Full circles, overlapping lives: Culture and generation in transition*. New York: Random House.

Hammad, S. (2003). *New York Times*. 3–24–03.

Horton, M. & Freire, P. (1990). *You make the road by walking: Conversations on education and social change*. Philadelphia: Temple University Press.

Kincheloe, J. (2000) In Soto, Lourdes D., *The politics of early childhood education*. New York: Peter Lang.

Russell, P. (1999). Personal interview. New York.

Steinberg, S. (2001). *Multi/intercultural conversations: A reader*. New York: Peter Lang.

Steinberg, S. & Kincheloe, J. (2001). Setting the context for critical multi/interculturalism: The power blocs of class elitism, white supremacy, and patriarchy. In Steinberg, S. *Multi/intercultural conversations: A reader*, pp. 3–30. New York: Peter Lang.

RETHINKING CHILDHOOD

JOE L. KINCHELOE & JANICE A. JIPSON, *General Editors*

A revolution is occurring regarding the study of childhood. Traditional notions of child development are under attack, as are the methods by which children are studied. At the same time, the nature of childhood itself is changing as children gain access to information once reserved for adults only. Technological innovations, media, and electronic information have narrowed the distinction between adults and children, forcing educators to rethink the world of schooling in this new context.

This series of textbooks and monographs encourages scholarship in all of these areas, eliciting critical investigations in developmental psychology, early childhood education, multicultural education, and cultural studies of childhood.

Proposals and manuscripts may be sent to the general editors:

> Joe L. Kincheloe
> c/o Peter Lang Publishing, Inc.
> 275 Seventh Avenue, 28th floor
> New York, New York 10001

To order other books in this series, please contact our Customer Service Department at:

> (800) 770-LANG (within the U.S.)
> (212) 647-7706 (outside the U.S.)
> (212) 647-7707 FAX

Or browse online by series at:
> www.peterlangusa.com